CAN I BE
YOUR GOD?

CAN I BE YOUR GOD?

an invitation

KAYLA A. KELLY

Kayla Kelly

To the hungry ones.

CONTENTS

Preface

The content of this book was birthed out of a time of trying to make sense of a situation, which many of us so often do. I was going back and forth between trusting God one minute, resulting in peace, and not trusting God the next minute, resulting in anxiety. Then God stopped me in my tracks and asked, "Am I your God or not?" This question was not asked in a condemning way but in one that lovingly challenged me to get off the fence and solidify what I believed about Him and His character. Subsequent questions came from Him such as:

- "Do you trust Me, or don't you trust Me?"
- "Am I leading you, or am I not leading you?"
- "Am I your provider, or am I not your provider?"
- "Am I in control, or am I not in control?"

In essence, God was asking me, "Who am I to you? Do you just know Me in the form of a 'name,' stating that I am Provider, Redeemer, Shepherd, and so on? Or do you also believe I am 'doing' and 'being' these names in your life? What side of the fence are you on?" From these revelations,

I started to write what it looks like to believe who God is in my life, not just as a noun but as a verb.

This book will take you on a journey of developing your relationship with God for the first time—similar to the process of two people meeting for a first date all the way through committing to each other in marriage—or it will help you renew and refresh your current relationship with Him. In each chapter, God will ask you, the reader, another question that will highlight a different character trait of Himself and how He wants to be that for you.

Every chapter will end with a section titled "God's Heart to You." This section is meant to help connect you even further with God so you can get to know His heart toward you and begin to experience Him speaking to you and you hearing His voice. The section will end with God asking you a question. I encourage you to not rush on to the next chapter before taking time to truly answer these questions, personally dialogue with God, and engage with what He is speaking and revealing to you.

I began writing this book at the beginning of 2018. With only 20 percent completed at the end of 2019 and through numerous promptings from God, I had a strong conviction to continue writing again and was determined to make this book a priority. In the spring of 2020, with an unforeseen job layoff and a worldwide pandemic that led to weeks of mandated quarantine and living by myself, there was no better time or opportunity to finish writing this book. I wrote the remaining 80 percent during this unique and unprecedented time. This book is a testament that God can create beauty from ashes and perhaps was meant for you to read and digest for such a time as this. Whether you don't believe in God, have fallen away from Him, believe in another spiritual being, or have been a Christian for a long time, the invitation from Him is the same for everyone: "Can I be your God?"

1

Can I Meet with You?

D o you remember the last time someone asked you "Can I meet with you?" You've likely been offered this invitation many times. It may have been your principal in grade school asking you to meet him in the office, a parent requesting you to come out of your bedroom for a discussion in the living room, a boss calling you to her office for an impromptu meeting, a potential client wanting to consult with you regarding your expertise, or a salesperson knocking on your door to ask if you have a few minutes to talk. This question often comes when you are least expecting it and when someone is awaiting an answer on the spot.

When someone asks to meet with you, you may feel cautious or reluctant, especially when you're unsure of what the meeting will be about or if the person is of high status or you have had very little history with them. You may be thinking,

"What will we talk about?"

"I'm nervous."
"Will it be awkward?"
"Am I in trouble?"
"I'm not sure I want to open up to them."
"Can I trust them?"
"I hope this goes well!"

Another reason you may feel uncomfortable meeting up with someone is that it involves nearness. That word *nearness* may leave you with the warm fuzzies or a chill down your spine. Why? Because it entails being close. It's intimate and vulnerable. It has a clear view. It leans in and narrows the divide. To some, this thought is inviting and welcoming. To others, it stiffens something inside them, and the urge to retreat is great.

Nearness with someone can be physical, emotional, mental, or spiritual. Some things you don't want near you because they are dangerous, threatening, or harmful, such as a rattlesnake or a person who is known to gossip. Other things you want near because they are satisfying, exciting, comforting, or life-giving, such as your best friend or your favorite meal.

Typically, you and I seek to control levels of nearness in order to self-protect. The default action is to guard or hide until you know it's safe to emerge. I imagine what you may have been using to accomplish this: It's handy and never far away. It's right at your disposal because you've likely used it many times. In fact, you're looking at it out of the corner of your eye. It's your custom-made shield.

You're wondering, *Is now the time to use it? Should I prop it up now before that thing, person, or situation gets too close? Before they see through my mask and see the real me? Maybe I'll keep it up just in case. What harm can come from keeping it up day after day? I can hide behind it, and when I have a surge of bravery, then I'll set it aside. When things get uncomfortable, I can retreat behind it again. What a great tool!*

The thing is, shields are meant to protect from harm, not to be used as permanent residences. Using the shield for a purpose for which it wasn't meant can actually cause more isolation than initially intended. You find yourself using it frequently and becoming comfortably cozy behind it. It was first used to protect from threats, but it can potentially keep good things out as well—preventing you from new relationships, adventures, job opportunities, thrilling experiences, and most importantly, being known.

> *Shields are meant to protect from harm, not to be used as permanent residences.*

In addition to the many good things that could be left out due to this seemingly protective shield, it can also leave you feeling disconnected from God. I understand why it's tempting to grab your shield at the thought of meeting with God or having a conversation with Him. Current and past experiences have made you feel uneasy about God, and you are unsure about meeting with Him for the first time or coming back to repair your strained relationship with Him. Or maybe much of your relationship with Him is good and strong but a specific area of your life is a little more painful than the rest, and you'd rather just keep it to yourself. You don't want to meet with Him about it. These reservations have caused you to keep your distance in hope of feeling safe and not being disappointed.

But God is not intimidated by your reluctancy, hesitancy, and fear.

I can imagine Him now, gently pursuing you without force or pressure, leaning in, not leaning away. He wishes that shield weren't there. He can get past it if He wants, but He sees your uncertain and doubtful heart behind the shield, and your heart is the prize. He's trying to come near you—not to condemn or scoff but to give. He wants to give you more than you can dare hope for and didn't know existed.

> *He's trying to come near you—not to condemn or scoff but to give.*

He is generous and wants to "add" to your life. Not only that, but He wants to show you who He is and not how the world has portrayed Him be.

He's also interested in you. He wants to hear from you and start connecting with you to develop a friendship. But none of this can happen without meeting together.

To truly get to know someone, information from a third party won't suffice. You'll eventually find a way to get near, to move closer, to meet with that person and talk face-to-face.

God desires for that shield to be lowered so you can see His face and He can see yours. There's no pressure or obligation attached to this meeting. It's an invitation. He's not demanding; He's asking. You have the freedom to RSVP yes or no to this invitation. But let me ask you—is there anything to gain by saying no? Is there anything to lose by saying yes?

Will you accept the invitation to meet with Him?

God's Heart to You

Though there's been a distance between you and Me, I want you to know that I am still here and I don't plan on leaving. Even when the distance persists, I continuously think of you. At times, you have forgotten about Me or have intentionally pushed Me out of your mind and heart with your shield. This pains Me.

I see you as lost treasure, a treasure I made and will find again. My desire to meet with you has never waned, and I will never stop pursuing a relationship with you. This could be a long chase, but I will do it. I don't get weary. I don't sleep. My love doesn't dampen or fade with time.

My desire is that for a moment you would lower your shield so I can look you in the eye. When you see My eyes, they will be full of delight, soft and not harsh. These eyes will be tear-filled as a result of the ache I have from not being let in. But they are also tears of joy because I have missed you.

May I come one step closer?

I know your heart. I know you have heard things about Me that aren't true, and many people have not represented Me well. I understand you don't want to be disappointed again. You think you are better off on your own and that the shield will keep you safe. I can tell you that shielding yourself from Me will not give you the desired outcome you are looking for. I have seen it with many others; they are left with an incomplete feeling, like they're missing something but can't quite pinpoint what it is. An ache that does not go away.

I want to be your shield. I want to be near you so I can protect you. I'm stronger than any man-made shield that's placed around your body, mind, or heart.

Can I come near? I can see your hesitancy.

I will ask again because you are worth My pursuit, can I come near to you? Even just a step closer?

Can I meet with you?

Can I meet with you?

☐ NO, I AM NOT QUITE READY TO MEET WITH YOU. I CAN'T SEEM TO LOWER MY SHIELD YET.

GOD: Thank you for being honest with Me. What is one of the main things that makes you feel uncomfortable meeting with Me? When you are ready, I am here. I will always be available to meet with you.

☐ YES, I AM WILLING AND WANTING TO MEET WITH YOU. THANK YOU FOR THE INVITATION!

GOD: This is wonderful! I can't wait to spend time with you. This is what we call the start of something new. I look forward to sitting in each other's presence and hearing what you have to say. I have things I want to say to you too.

2

Can I Hear What You Have to Say?

E very day, all around you, people have thoughts and opinions they want to express to you. With many voices swirling all around, listening has become increasingly difficult. Attention spans have dwindled to minutes, at most. You find yourself antsy and fidgety as you watch a commercial or listen to a customer's opinion or how a friend's weekend went. You want to move on to the next thing. Or you might pretend to listen and nod your head, having no clue what they just said. Maybe you can recite a few facts, but is there any awareness of what that person was really trying to get across or how they felt?

If you and I are being honest, there are times we don't genuinely care because we don't want to hear more than we have to. We don't want their burdens and sometimes not even their triumphs. We'd rather get our point across and move along. We have things to do, places to go, and people to see. "Let's be efficient. Let's save it for another day.

They'll be fine," we say to ourselves. We are not terrible people when we think or do these things; often we respond this way simply because we are tired, have hit our limit for the day, or are struggling with our own burdens and stressors.

In general, though, it's safe to say that listening has become a lost art. How often have you seen on social media or had someone ask you, "Can I hear what you have to say?" Perhaps your family, friends, or colleagues will occasionally ask you this question either in passing or in a genuine sit-down conversation. Or maybe no one has ever asked you this question. You strive to find that sliver of an opening in a conversation to interject your thoughts or even interrupt if it comes to it. When this question isn't asked, it's a loss for all parties. So many words have never been spoken or brought to life because this question was never asked.

When you ask someone, "Can I hear what you have to say?" you are conveying to them that they have value and something rich to offer. They may know something or have words of wisdom you may not have and never would have known without this question. And when someone doesn't ask to hear what you have to say, they're also missing out on knowing you, your perspective, and your heart.

> *Listening is more than hearing "words." It's a leaning in. It's a focus.*

Listening is more than hearing "words." It's a leaning in. It's a focus. It's a genuine desire to know this person better. Words are a reflection of what's going on in one's heart and mind. When you seek to listen, you are really seeking to know them. You are more equipped to respond because now you can truly see and hear what those words actually mean. What do their words convey about who they are and the message they are trying to get across? Is frustration, hurt, or anger behind those words? Are they words of hope or words of anxiety or fearfulness? Are they carefree, lighthearted, or joyful? Are their many words saying they are hungry for someone to finally listen and understand them?

You may not have felt heard throughout your life by parents, teachers, friends, or co-workers. You may feel like not many people really want to hear what you have to say and get to know the real you. I guarantee you are not the only one who has experienced this or feels this way.

But there is One who, more than anyone else, is eager to hear from you. God, every day, is asking you, "Can I hear what you have to say?" He's not asking out of obligation or duty. He doesn't have a stopwatch saying, "Okay, you have five minutes. Spit it out quickly; I have a busy schedule, so chop-chop." I've been guilty of having this attitude with others. But, thank goodness, God doesn't treat us this way.

He already knows what's going on in your mind and heart. It's not a mystery for Him. But if He already knows, why does He want you to say it? Because that is what relationship looks like. A good friendship is not a one-way show where one person talks and the other has nothing to contribute. Both have value, both have things to say, and both listen intently. Both care.

God loves to listen. He's good at it, and it pleases Him to do so. He says many times in the Bible to call on Him, to pray to Him, to present your requests to Him, and to seek Him.

> *God loves to listen. He's good at it, and it pleases Him to do so.*

Morning, noon, and night
I cry out in my distress,
and the LORD hears my voice.
– Psalm 55:17 (NLT)

I love the LORD because he hears my voice
and my prayer for mercy. Because he bends
down to listen, I will pray as long as I have
breath!
– Psalm 116:1–2 (NLT)

The LORD is near to all who call on him,
to all who call on him in truth.
– Psalm 145:18

You and I are not used to "no restrictions" when it
comes to someone listening, but God has more than enough
capacity to listen to you and your concerns. He doesn't have
time constraints. Nor does He get fidgety, agitated, or im-
patient. He never gets offended by what you're saying, and
He doesn't get confused or overwhelmed. There's no right or
wrong time or place to talk to Him.

Do you talk to God about your day? Have you ex-
pressed your doubts about His character to Him? Have you
inquired about all the "whys" or asked for something versus
complained or worried? Do you thank
Him for all the blessings you've experienced? He wants to hear it all—the
good, the bad, and the ugly.

I encourage you to talk to Him
like you talk to a good friend. Noth-

> *He wants to
> hear it all—the
> good, the bad,
> and the ugly.*

ing is off-limits. Big or small. Lighthearted or burdensome. Observations or needing clarity. Thanksgiving or frustrations. Speak it all to Him—He's waiting to hear from you.

God's Heart to You

Listening to you is a joy for Me. I am here and in no hurry. Time is not an issue for Me. I'm all ears. I will plant myself here as long as you need Me. Take your time.

How have you been? What's on your heart? What are you worried about? What are you scared of? What are your desires?

Your thoughts and perspectives are not hidden from Me. I can handle anything you have to say. Please don't stop short, only telling Me facts or giving Me the abridged version. I want to hear your heart—your emotions, your hurt and pain, your excitement, your dreams. If you're doubting My character or goodness, please tell Me. Tell Me everything. It's okay if it's the same issues as last week—I'll hear them again.

I want to listen to you because I can offer you peace and wisdom simply because I love and care about you. There are no strings attached. Just a pure love and interest in you. I know that is hard to take in because you may have not experienced this before. I know many have overlooked you and not valued your thoughts, opinions, and expertise. But I'm different. I'm genuinely interested and want to hear it all.

And know that while you are pouring your heart out to Me, I feel with you. My heart aches when your heart aches. If you don't want to speak but just cry, that's okay too. I feel sorrow as tears are running down your cheeks. I hear and know what those tears are saying. I also rejoice as you tell Me how someone blessed you or how you blessed someone else.

I'm not just ears. I'm heart too. Again, no rush. Know that I care and that I want to tend to your heart. I am eagerly and patiently waiting.

Can I hear what you have to say?

Can I hear what you have to say?

☐ NO, I DON'T FEEL COMFORTABLE TELLING YOU
WHAT IS ON MY MIND AND HEART YET. I'M NOT
READY TO OPEN UP.

GOD: Is there something keeping you from wanting to speak with Me? You can be honest. When you are ready to talk, I am here to listen.

☐ YES, I AM WILLING AND READY TO TELL YOU
WHAT IS ON MY MIND AND HEART. THANK YOU
FOR LISTENING TO ME.

GOD: Thank you for trusting Me with what you are about to express. I am listening. After hearing what you have to say, I would enjoy engaging in conversation with you in response to what is on your heart.

3

Can I Tell You Something?

Many people in the world have a lot to say about a lot of things. We've all listened to people who have "something to say," whether it's a spouse, parent, friend, boss, teacher, client, singer, actor, or a stranger. Sometimes you wonder, "Is what they are saying true?" "Are they exaggerating?" "Is this important? If so, maybe I should lean in and focus more." Let's be honest, at times you and I wonder when their story or explanation will be over, because it's not always relevant or of interest.

People will use a variety of methods to get their voices heard—from billboards and commercials to social media to junk mail to a town hall meeting—all to get your attention and tell you something extremely "important." From their perspective, what they have to say is pertinent, and they will do almost anything to get you to listen. With their advice or product, they believe they can change your life! And it can, just not always in the way you thought it would. Sometimes after listening to what they have to say, you learn, grow, and gain clarity. Other times you leave feeling disheartened, unsettled, or confused.

What and whom you choose to listen to is a game changer. Who has your ear? What voices and messages are getting your attention? Some words that approach your ears are full of truth, are valuable, and add to your life. Other words distort, lie, and get you off course.

What you allow into your eyes and ears will seep into your mind and heart. What's in your mind and heart will overflow into your actions. In essence, your actions are a reflection of what you allow in your body and soul. Choose wisely, my friend!

Amid all the noise, something else is seeking your attention. It's one of a kind and unlike any other voice. It's not only the voice of reason but the voice of truth. It's a voice that gets you back on the right path so your purpose can be fulfilled. A voice that soothes you when all the other voices—sometimes including your own—confuse you. A voice that both thunders and whispers, full of strength and tenderness. It oozes with love.

> *A voice that both thunders and whispers, full of strength and tenderness. It oozes with love. It's the voice of God.*

It's the voice of God.

His voice tells you who you are and who He is. Other voices try to interject and tell you who you should be or how you don't quite measure up or where to find your worth and success. They will paint a different picture of who God is than who He says He is. Some of these dissuading voices are clever and will weave in little truths, just enough for you to grab hold of and believe them.

So how do you discern between His voice and all the others? One of the main ways He speaks to you is through His Word, the Bible. He also speaks to you through the Holy Spirit, which will be elaborated on a little later.

You may ask, "What makes the Bible so special? Isn't it just another book? An old book? Is it even relevant? How can you put so much stock in this one book when there are so many other good books and resources to glean from?"

The Bible is different than any other book in that it was inspired by God Himself and not humans.

> All Scripture is inspired by God.
> – 2 Timothy 3:16 (NLT)

Hard to comprehend? Yes, I'm right there with you. Humans wrote it, but God worked and spoke through them. The Bible was written by about forty different authors over a span of about two thousand years. These authors spoke different languages, lived in different countries, had a variety of occupations and socioeconomic statuses, and most never met each other. God's Word is full of specific dates, locations, names, and genealogies. If the Bible were made up, the writers wouldn't have included these specific items because they can all be traced back or referenced to. Many times, an event was predicted and came to pass hundreds of years later.

Today we can easily do an online search to learn what people said and did hundreds of years ago. However, these writers couldn't text, call, or email to make sure their stories and dates lined up. There wasn't a library to check out a history book or a documentary they could watch on television.

And yet, the message among all these authors, over a great period of time, has a theme that is threaded through the entire book. What is this theme? Throughout the Bible, it tells us who God is and who we are and demonstrates His consistent love and pursuit of us.

God's words are more than statements on a page, like a school's textbook. They are meant to reach and connect with you on a heart level and speak something special—just for *you*.

> Your word is a lamp for my feet,
> a light on my path.
> – Psalm 119:105

And look at Hebrews 4:12 (NLT):

> For the word of God is alive and powerful. It
> is sharper than the sharpest two-edged sword,
> cutting between soul and spirit, between
> joint and marrow. It exposes our innermost
> thoughts and desires.

> *The Word is alive. Alive! It moves. It reaches. It engages. It inspires. It lifts.*

The Word is alive. Alive! It moves. It reaches. It engages. It inspires. It lifts. These words are active and relevant, both today and tomorrow, across all countries and cultures. These words are more than words on a page—they do something to your heart, mind, and soul that other words don't have the ability to do.

We hear a lot of chatter from day to day through many different avenues. Most chatter, if never heard, likely wouldn't have any impact on your life. How many conversations have you been a part of that were fruitless or in some cases damaging? Think of the many times you've overheard gossip, rumors, and complaining. How did that impact those who participated? I'm guessing they did not walk away encouraged or inspired.

If you're not regularly reading God's Word, it will be hard to recognize His voice when He's speaking to you. Gossip and rumors, arguing and blaming, sarcasm and scolding, white lies, complaining, and pessimism are constantly swirling around you. These things are so intertwined in our culture it's easy to not recognize them. If you're not in tune with God's voice, you will fall prey to thinking that is what His voice sounds like too. Find the antonym to each of those words, and that will likely be more in line with what His voice sounds like.

The Bible often refers to us as sheep, with God as our shepherd. Sheep are prone to wander and are vulnerable to predators without the guidance and protection of their shepherd. Sheep that spend numerous hours and days with their shepherd develop such an intimate and trustworthy relationship with him that they will only respond to his voice, ignoring all others. The same is true for you. If you know the Shepherd's voice, you can follow Him and remain under His care and protection: "When he was brought out all his own, he goes on ahead of them, and

If you know the Shepherd's voice, you can follow Him and remain under His care and protection.

his sheep follow him because they know his voice. But they will never follow a stranger; in fact, they will run away from him because they do not recognize a stranger's voice" (John 10:4–5).

Psalm 19:7–10 (TPT) describes more benefits to reading, listening to, and following His voice:

> God's Word is perfect in every way;
> how it revives our souls!
> His laws lead us to truth,
> and his ways change the simple into wise.
> His teachings make us joyful and
> radiate his light;
> his precepts are so pure!
> His commands, how they challenge us to
> keep close to his heart!
> The revelation-light of his word makes my
> spirit shine radiant.
> Every one of the Lord's commands is right;
> following them brings cheer.
> Nothing he says ever needs to be changed.
> The rarest treasures of life are found
> in his truth.
> That's why I prize God's word like others
> prize the finest gold.
> Nothing brings the soul such sweetness
> as seeking his living words.

God wants to speak to you because He loves you. He's not bossy and controlling like many think He is, but He will add life to you like the above passage states. He knows your past, your personality, and your current circumstances. He has a way of speaking to you that comforts, encourages, and emboldens you—not only every day but in the moment you need it most. Often, others don't know what to say when you're hurting, confused, or when you simply need some life advice. I'm sure you have said these words or have heard them from another: "I'm sorry, I just don't have the words," or "I'm speechless." With God, you don't have to worry about false motives, deception, or the runaround. But you can trust His Word at face value.

You have started to talk to Him and tell Him what's on your mind. Now, will you let Him speak to you?

God's Heart to You

I've been loving hearing from you recently, and I love speaking to you too. This is called <u>relationship</u>, and it is so sweet when it's a two-way street. Rest assured, I hear all the other voices the world is speaking to you, and I understand the stress and confusion you are experiencing. Countless voices from every angle tell you to go this way, believe this, focus over here—voices that whisper, "I'm irrelevant. I don't exist. I'm not worth knowing. You can't trust me." They tell you that you need to look and act a certain way to be accepted. They say, "Keep striving. Don't fall behind. Succeed. Take care of yourself. Focus on what you can see, and follow your own heart."

Oh, does My voice sing a different tune! Can I tell you something? I am love. And I love you. Why would I want to listen and speak to you if I didn't care about you? You are not a bother. I want you near. I delight in you and want to sing over you with the sweetest lyrics. I want you to trust that I am for you and not against you. I am advocating for you! My words will lead and guide you, comfort and encourage you, set you free from undue burdens. I want to keep reminding you of who I am, because when you believe and remember who I am, a peace will flood your heart. You can let go and trust. And not only peace but a boldness and a new-found purpose because I know you and made you. My words will empower you!

Again, I am for you. One of my greatest desires is for my voice to be the loudest and sweetest in your life. My voice is not just letters on a page, but my Spirit will speak and lead you into a canyon of wisdom that will take you places in your heart and mind and in this world that you didn't even know were there. I will carry you through this life with My love and My voice.

Read, listen, and meditate on My words.

Can I tell you something?

Can I tell you something?

☐ No, I feel uneasy about what You might say to me. I'm not ready to start conversing.

GOD: Are you nervous or fearful about what I'm going to say to you? If so, why? Remember, your voice matters to Me and I am open to listening to you anytime along the way. When you are ready to have a conversation, I am here.

☐ Yes, I am open and ready to hear what You have to say!

GOD: I'm excited to share with you many things about your uniqueness and who I want to be for you. Also, there is something else I'd love to talk to you about next—what love is and about the love I have for you.

4

Can I Love You to Pieces?

ove. Such a loaded word. It's a word used to describe feelings about pizza, designer shoes, hobbies, and relationships. Love, as a word and an action, has become so diluted over time that it has become difficult to recognize in its genuine form. Every person yearns for it. No one has said, "I don't want to be loved and cared for. I want to be deserted and hated on. I want to be neglected and mistreated." Deep in your soul, you want to be loved whether you know how to articulate it or not. It's because you were made to love and be loved, and when you are not, you feel the pain and emptiness.

When you don't feel loved, it leaves a gaping hole inside, and the emptiness it leaves is palpable. This hole was not meant to remain empty but to be filled. But when that hole lies there void, the temptation is to fill it with almost anything that happens to come across your path in order to relieve some of the pain you feel. Like finding a pothole in the road, someone or something is sought out to fill it because it was not meant to remain empty. It's comparable to a vacant position at a company that needs to be filled to operate efficiently. Or like a fresh cut or injury that's tended to by being stitched up or by putting on a bandage.

When pain exists, you want to fix it, mend it, heal it, and do anything to lessen the pain. Emotional pain is just as real as physical pain. Not being or feeling loved can leave you, as they say, heartbroken or with a heartache.

> *When you feel unloved, the involuntary response is to earn it somehow.*

When you feel unloved, the involuntary response is to earn it somehow. You think:

- If I did less bad things to make that person angry, then they would love me more or hate me less.
- If I was more accomplished in school or in my career, then they would look favorably on me.
- If I had won that award, I would have received their applause.
- If I were prettier or more handsome like so-and-so, they would be drawn to me and not overlook me.
- If I had a more dynamic personality, they would want to converse with me and bring me around their friends.
- If I hadn't messed up or gone down the wrong path, they wouldn't have left me.

What "ifs" are you telling yourself? In what ways do you feel like you need to "be more" to deserve love? Who do you wish would love you? Who in your life do you feel loved by, and how does that person demonstrate that love to you?

There's good reason many people have a skewed idea of

what love is and what it looks like. Some people in your life say they love you, and you feel and experience it. Others say they love you, and their actions and words don't reflect what you think love should look like. So, what is love, *really*?

You've seen love reflected many different ways and have heard various definitions, but let me present another definition to you. This is the definition of love the Bible gives to you and me:

> If I speak in the tongues of men or of angels,
> but do not have love,
> I am only a resounding gong
> or a clanging cymbal.
> If I have the gift of prophecy and can fathom
> all mysteries and all knowledge,
> and if I have a faith that can
> move mountains,
> but do not have love, I am nothing.
> If I give all I possess to the poor and give over
> my body to hardship that I may boast,
> but do not have love, I gain nothing.
> Love is patient, love is kind.
> It does not envy, it does not boast,
> it is not proud.
> It does not dishonor others,
> it is not self-seeking,
> it is not easily angered,
> it keeps no record of wrongs.
> Love does not delight in evil
> but rejoices with the truth.

It always protects, always trusts, always hopes,
always perseveres.
– 1 Corinthians 13:1–7

So, this passage is saying that I can be a ten out of ten in my speech, prophecy, knowledge, faith, giving, and serving, and it could still add up to nothing? That nothing will have been gained, even with this hall of fame list of accomplishments?

Amazingly, people can be the recipient of all these great acts and yet still feel unloved. People feel truly loved when verses 4–7 are played out. Can you imagine someone being gentle and kind to you? Not feeling a hint of envy toward you but genuinely celebrating you? Not having any anger or resentment toward you or going back in history and re-hashing all the ways you messed up? Being able to believe everything they say because it's all true? And with all their might protecting you, trusting you, hoping in and for you, and persevering in developing their relationship with you? And doing all those things all the time for you?

Now think about loving not only your best friend this way but your greatest enemy—that person who intention-ally caused you harm, the last person you want to spend time with. The person you love avoiding. To love this kind of person feels almost unbearable. And if you did attempt to love this person, it would likely be done begrudgingly or while dragging your feet. Would it be love then?

Now check out this love:

This is how much God loved the world:
He gave his Son, his one and only Son.

And this is why: so that no one need be
destroyed; by believing in him, anyone can
have a whole and lasting life. God didn't go
to all the trouble of sending his Son merely
to point an accusing finger, telling the world
how bad it was. He came to help, to put the
world right again.
— John 3:16–17 (MSG)

For the joy set before him he endured the
cross, scorning its shame, and sat down at the
right hand of the throne of God.
— Hebrews 12:2

God so loved the world. Who is the world? Everyone.
Take a minute to think of who everyone is. Your list may
include your nice neighbors, family, friends, coworkers,
people who cut you off in traffic, atheists, Christians, ter-
rorists, and everyone in between. He loved and loves them
all. Amazing. God loved them so much that He *gave*. He
gave His Son, Jesus, to you. Why? For your good, so that
you could have meaning, purpose, and freedom here on
earth apart from earning it from those
around you. It's so that you wouldn't
have to wear shame and condemnation. It's so you could have abundant
life here on earth as well as a life that
goes on and on with Him after your
time here is over.

> *He loved them
> so much
> that He
> gave.*

Did He have to do this? No. Did He do it out of obligation or begrudgingly? No. He did it because *He is love.* It's what and who He is.

Not only was Jesus crucified on a cross by His enemies to take the penalty and sting of your sin but He endured it. He didn't just get through dying on the cross. Remember 1 Corinthians 13:3? Jesus didn't just merely sacrifice His life because it was enjoyable or He had nothing better to do. His sacrifice was wrapped in love. His love was put into action.

> *His sacrifice was wrapped in love.*

Jesus at one point said, "Father, if you are willing, take this cup from me; yet not my will, but yours be done" (Luke 22:42). Jesus was obedient to God because God can be trusted and does everything out of love. God's love for you and the "joy set before him [Jesus]" was the driving force behind the walk to the cross. In the middle of the pain and what seemed like a tragedy to many, He knew there was freedom on the other side. Love led the way.

No one on earth has loved me like this. Has anyone loved you like this? Most are just happy when someone doesn't forget their birthday.

He loves differently.

He loves without condition.

He loves fully.

He loves fiercely.

He loves perfectly.

He is love.

God's Heart to You

I want to first say that My heart hurts for how the world has "loved" you. I see how conditional and superficial it is and how it has left you underwhelmed and unsatisfied. I'm sorry for the lack of love you have and are experiencing in your marriage or in your singleness, from strangers and even from your confidants. It wasn't meant to be this way. I not only want to fill in the gap but fill you up so that you are beaming, almost to the point of giddiness, even when the world is against you or their love simply falls short.

I know you completely and still love you. I know there are times you feel unlovable and that you are not enough. Your actions and past mistakes do not deter My love. My love is a flaming arrow; nothing can stop it or get in its way. It pierces through that shield you like to use, drills through mountains, and is unhindered by depression. My love is hard to accept and understand because it's unlike any other love. My love will take the messiest of situations and create beauty from them. It knows no bounds and has no limits. It perseveres and perseveres and perseveres. And then perseveres some more.

Sometimes My love may not look like love, just as a parent creates healthy boundaries because they want to protect their children from what they cannot see. Sometimes a parent doesn't share every piece of information because they know the child wouldn't understand or be able to handle the weight of the news. A parent at times lovingly disciplines a child so he or she larns the difference between good and bad. None of these things look or feel pleasing to the child, but it's all for their good. My love is similar. Although you may not have experienced perfect love from your parents, My love is demonstrated perfectly toward you.

Trust My love for you even when it may not make sense or always look like love. Sometimes I may not give you exactly what you're asking for because I have something sweeter for you, and it wouldn't be My kind of love to give you an imperfect gift. And My love is not something you earn from Me—it's a gift to you.

I love loving you.

I enjoy loving you.

I don't have to love you; I want to love you.

I love you dearly.

Will you believe this?

Will you receive this?

Can I love you to pieces?

Can I love you to pieces?

☐ No, I'm not ready for You to love me to pieces. I'm still struggling to understand and accept this kind of love.

GOD: Have you ever felt let down by My love? If so, in what ways? Know that even if You don't feel ready or comfortable receiving My love and care for you, My love still remains for you because it is who I am and I can't go against My character. You have the freedom to express your doubts to Me.

☐ Yes, I want to experience Your kind of love. You can love me to pieces.

GOD: Thank you for being open to receiving My love. It means more to Me than you know. You will begin to be more aware of all the small ways as well as the big ways I have loved you in the past and am doing so at this moment. Along with Me loving you unconditionally, I also want you to be free. Let the road to freedom begin...

5

Can I Make You Free as a Bird?

*P*erfect: "Complete and correct in every way, of the best possible type or without fault."[1] You probably have people in your life who seem to be perfect. There's a natural desire to be like them and emulate them. It's easy to see hundreds of flaws and weaknesses in yourself, and you think if those things were gone, and you could be perfect, then you would be more liked and successful and less distraught.

But you and I know that perfection is an illusion. No one can attain it, yet we all strive for it. Imperfection does not sit well with us. When we make a mistake at work, forget to pay a bill, relapse into old habits, relive past regrets, or have broken relationships, we can be very hard on ourselves. We think, *I shouldn't be struggling with this. I should have it more together by now.*

So you strive and strive to be better, trying to compen-

---

[1] Cambridge Dictionary, s.v. "perfect," accessed October 4, 2020, https://dictionary.cambridge.org/dictionary/english/perfect.

sate for your faults and imperfections. You try to do more good things, volunteer, work extra hours, or even punish yourself in some way to make up for what you perceive to be a lack in who you are. This leads to perpetual unrest and never feeling good enough.

> *Perfectionism is a weight, like a bird trying to fly with mud on its wings.*

Perfectionism is a weight, like a bird trying to fly with mud on its wings. The height to which it can fly is restricted. The distance it can go is limited. Its flight is wobbly. This unnecessary weight does the bird no favors. You think it would be silly and foolish for the bird to keep the mud on its wings, and yet this is what you and I do to ourselves every day. We work toward losing physical pounds, but we add additional emotional and mental burdens to ourselves routinely.

The culture you live in plays a role in adding weight and pressure to your life too. There's a multitude of rules and expectations you try to live up to from bosses, parents, teachers, neighbors, and children. You don't want to disappoint them. You don't want to fail.

Think of the times you received grades in school. If you got all the answers right on a test, you got an A, and A students get awards. They get recognition and applause. But C students don't. Is the A student more important or significant? Do they have greater worth than the C student? No, but the world often acts as though they do. In many cases, awards and recognition are a great thing, but over time, you can start to believe you are less than, insignificant, not good enough, or lack potential because you may not meet certain standards that come at you from different areas of life. Both

A and C students are worthy of love and attention, have unique gifts and skills, and have much to offer the world. Both are worth fighting for. Each and every person is!

What would it feel like if you were loved and celebrated with no strings attached? That is hard to imagine.

Whether it be from the world or from yourself, you feel the constant weight of doing things right, being good enough, and measuring up. You feel the weight of your weaknesses, mistakes, failures, regrets, and sins. Guilt and shame sit on your shoulders like a backpack full of rocks.

You weren't meant to operate day to day heavy laden, to feel like you are dragging around a ball and chain or just getting through the day, getting through life.

You were meant to be free.

You were meant to be full of hope.

You were meant to pour out, not left gasping for air.

You were meant to be free.

What is the opposite of life? Death.

When you live a life loving what God hates and hating what God loves, you sin—not against a "thing" but against Him. When you intentionally choose to sin and live in sin, you feel anything but alive. There may be a temporary thrill or exhilaration, but it doesn't last long.

Sin forms a divide between you and God. To close that divide, there is a cost. Anytime something is broken, it costs something to fix it; the same is true with a broken relationship with God. The wages, or cost, of our sin is death.

Before Jesus was born, people had to sacrifice animals to pay the cost of their sin and to get right with God. This was a continual practice. Every time sin entered, a sacrifice was needed. Jesus came to be the ultimate and final sacrifice.

> *On the cross, Jesus said, "It is finished." This means there's no more trying to get right with God.*

On the cross, Jesus said, "It is finished." This means there's no more trying to get right with God. He paid the price for your past, present, and future sins. It's on Him, not you. It's Jesus who fills the divide; it's He who washes the mud off your wings.

Because of this, He sees you as pure and clean. You are no longer a slave to sin—it doesn't have control over you any longer. Your sin no longer defines you; He does. It's so easy to be defined and labeled by what you have done: liar, cheater, thief, adulterer, murderer, etc. But when you live in communion with Him, any label you give yourself falls off. It can't stick because of what He did for you. Your new label is now *son* or *daughter*.

It's His grace that allows this. Grace is getting what we don't deserve. And it's by faith we believe and receive this undeserved gift. We get to live free while on earth and get to spend eternity with Him.

The old way of striving, living for self, and earning love is gone. The new way of trusting Him, serving others, and resting in His love is here. As we stay close to Him, the old continues to fade, and the new continues to appear.

> Therefore, if anyone is in Christ, the new
> creation has come: The old has gone, the new
> is here!
> – 2 Corinthians 5:17

Even though you become new and are being transformed by Him, there is no getting around the pain, temptation, and trials you will experience during your lifetime. You will fall short at times, and others will mistreat you. All this has and will come. But these hardships will not overtake you, and you are promised help and peace in the storms.

> We are hard pressed on every side, but not crushed; perplexed, but not in despair; persecuted, but not abandoned; struck down, but not destroyed. We always carry around in our body the death of Jesus, so that the life of Jesus may also be revealed in our body.
> – 2 Corinthians 4:8–10

I don't know what you're going through or what your year or even your lifetime has been like. You may be feeling defeated and have lost all hope. You may feel like you're standing in a deep pit, in the darkest of graves.

Do something crazy—lie down in that grave. Surrender. Not to death but to Him.

As you reach up to take His hand, leave your old life lying on the grave's floor.

He is about to do something new in you and for you.

Rescue and freedom are ahead.

Life and joy are ahead.

Peace and provision are ahead.

Let Jesus wash the mud off your wings and get ready to soar!

God's Heart to You

I know there are so many things weighing on your heart these days, and it saddens Me to see you in this state. Your heart is anxious, and your feet feel weighted. You are wondering how you will get through this season and how much longer you can manage this struggle.

For a moment, will you lift up your head, so we can talk?

This is not the life I have for you. I am not the one to fill you with shame and hopelessness. That is from My great enemy. I don't treat you as he treats you. He comes to take and steal from you. I come to give and bless. I have more for you, and I want to bring it to you.

To give you the abundant life I have planned for you, we need to get rid of all that is separating you and me—all the sin. I will remove the dark cloud this sin has hovering over you. You don't have to carry the burden of your past one minute longer. Let Me remove the old; you don't need that anymore. You don't have to strive to make yourself right and clean. Let My son Jesus do that. That is what He died for—to take it upon Himself so you can walk freely. There's no earning involved; this freedom and eternal life are gifts from Me to you. When you accept these gifts, it will feel like you're soaring on the wings of eagles.

Make room for the new thing I am about to do in your life.

When you get scared of the trouble this world brings, take heart! I have already overcome the world. It is no match for Me.

I will give you peace.

I will wash the mud off your wings.

I will take you to new heights.

Can I make you free as a bird?

Can I make you free as a bird?

☐ No. In a strange way, I feel comfortable staying in the familiar and with how I've been living. I'm not ready to release the things I've been carrying. Change and introducing new things sometimes makes me nervous.

God: I understand wanting to feel safe. Staying in the familiar can feel like safety, but it can also lead you to feeling stuck. And I don't want that for you. I have great plans for you, and I want you to experience all I have for you. Next time you're outside, observe the birds, the ones without mud on their wings.

☐ YES, I WANT TO BE FREE FROM MY OLD WAY OF LIVING AND STRIVING TO BE GOOD ENOUGH. I'M READY FOR THE NEW THINGS YOU HAVE IN STORE FOR ME!

God: It is My joy to set you free and renew your spirit. I'm excited to see you flourish! I have even more for you, like wanting to make you powerful and wise. Let me explain more...

6

Can I Make You Powerful and Wise?

We are in awe of power. We admire the superhero that saves the day or the impressive strength of an elite athlete and marvel at the sound of roaring thunder. Power is often rewarded and revered. When you look at your home life, work status, or physical stature, you may or may not feel very powerful. Or at least, it's not the word many would use to describe you and me.

You've likely watched movies where the characters are seen enjoying their use of power. You may have watched a scene of an overdemanding CEO of a company or a sports coach who likes to have control over the people they are leading or a powerful villain trying to take over the world. Or you've seen movies with characters using their power for good, like Batman and Spiderman. As in real life, there are powerful people you run from due to fear of harm and other powerful people you run toward for safety and security.

What category would you put yourself in? With your

power, influence, or position, do you find people running toward you or away from you?

Similar to power, knowledge is often rewarded and revered. Being smart can make you feel good about yourself, especially when you can spew out random facts that very few know. Others stand in awe saying, "Wow, how did you know that?" Knowledge also has a sense of power because if you can outsmart someone, you can win the debate and walk away as the winner. We've seen this played out numerous times on cable news or in a classroom or on social media. Knowledge is also powerful in that it can help create a new invention, solve problems, and understand how things operate. Knowledge is a good thing if it is used appropriately, and that is where wisdom comes into play.

You've heard the phrase "wisdom comes with age." That's true—partially. As you get older, you've gone through life experiences, trials, and mistakes that have shaped and challenged you. Many learn, grow, and develop from these experiences, but not all do. Have you ever met an older person you would never take advice from because of their bitterness, their communication, or the decisions they have made over the years? Have you ever met a young person who seems "wise beyond their years" or has an "old soul"? Wisdom spans all ages. Wisdom is discerning what to do with the knowledge you have. It also recognizes if certain knowledge or information is right or true.

Wisdom and power can do great things when working together. Like paint colors, they are beautiful on their own, but when mixed, they create something that much more beautiful, appealing, and impactful.

Is there someone in your life you would describe as powerful and wise? What has their impact been in their home, workplace, and community? It's very likely that they are admired and esteemed by many.

As powerful, knowledgeable, and wise as you may already be, it unfortunately often falls short. The reality is there will be times when you feel powerless to change a particular situation. There will be information left to learn or you'll be confused on how to handle a challenging circumstance. But the great news is that God equips you in ways you are not able to do on your own. He has given you another person to hear from, glean from, and rely on. He is the Holy Spirit. If you decide to turn toward God, accepting Jesus's love and forgiveness, and decide to live for and with Him, the Holy Spirit comes and resides in you. It is a miracle beyond comprehension. From that moment on, your life on earth—and after earth—is forever changed.

> *He has given you another person to hear from, glean from, and rely on. He is the Holy Spirit.*

The Holy Spirit offers perfect power and wisdom in and through you, all day, every day. His wisdom often looks countercultural and can even be seen as foolish by some because wisdom isn't the same as logic. Sometimes He leads you in a direction that's not logical but is better than anything you could have thought up or strategized on your own. He sees and knows things you and I can't.

If someone needed advice, and they set up two meetings, one with a person who has the Holy Spirit and one who does not, those two meetings would likely look different.

Advice without the Holy Spirit's counsel and direction has the potential to be misleading, even though it seems right in that person's eyes. Advice from the Holy Spirit is wise and fruitful. Since the Holy Spirit knows your heart intimately, He has just the right words for your unique situation— maybe words you were not expecting or even wanting to hear, but words that are for your (and others') ultimate good, words that bring hope, healing, and encouragement, setting you back on the path He created in advance for you to walk in.

Many would love to have a full-time therapist who goes with them everywhere to have on-demand advice and direction at any time and at no cost. Sign me up! Well, that is what the Holy Spirit does. He's your perfect counselor and constant helper. He gives you discernment when you are confused and don't know if you should step to the left or right, what job to take, how to handle a rebellious child, where to allocate your finances, and everything else you're unsure how to handle.

He knows your heart, mind, and motives. He lovingly lets you know when you've done, said, or thought something that wasn't honorable to Him and others. The Holy Spirit does not condemn and shame. He is not waving His finger at you. He doesn't turn His back on you. He doesn't scold. If you hear shameful thoughts or feel deserted by Him, that is not His voice, and those are not His actions. Satan wants to weigh you down so you can't be free or do what God has called you to do. The Holy Spirit gently and lovingly convicts you. It's His kindness that leads you to repentance.

Now the Lord is the Spirit, and where the
Spirit of the Lord is, there is freedom.
– 2 Corinthians 3:17

There is freedom with the Holy Spirit. Freedom from what? From guilt and shame hanging over your head from your past or that thing you know you shouldn't have done two hours ago. Instead, He removes the shackles of regret and allows you to walk away from those things with confidence. You have freedom from feeling purposeless, worthless, and hopeless—freedom from sitting in confusion, depression, and anxiety. The Holy Spirit brings clarity and direction. No longer must you walk aimlessly. He leads you into freedom from old mindsets, old habits, old perspectives, and old aims. He brings the new.

> *He leads you into freedom from old mindsets, old habits, old perspectives, and old aims.*

As the Holy Spirit takes away the old and brings on the new, you will notice newness not only on the inside of you but also on the outside. What you ingest from watching TV, reading social media, books, and magazines, or from the many voices you hear throughout the day affects your heart and mind. The Holy Spirit is your filter. He reminds you of what God has said in His Word. He helps you discern if something is truth or a lie. The things you take in can change you for better or worse depending on if you listen to the Holy Spirit's guidance. The Spirit changes you from the inside out. Whatever is in you will come out of you through your words and actions. If you're allowing the Holy Spirit to be your teacher and discerner, you will, no doubt, bear good fruit.

> But the fruit of the Spirit is love, joy, peace,
> forbearance, kindness, goodness, faithfulness,
> gentleness and self-control.
> – Galatians 5:22–23

Do you want to be known for those qualities? Do you want to exude these traits in your home? With your family and friends? Neighbors? At your workplace? To the cashier or server? These outward qualities don't appear without the Holy Spirit first doing a work in you and me.

As the Holy Spirit makes you wise and transforms you from the inside out, He also empowers you to perform miraculous deeds through Him. Jesus says in John 14:12 (TPT),

> "I tell you this timeless truth: The person
> who follows me in faith, believing in me, will
> do the same mighty miracles that I do—even
> greater miracles than these because I go to be
> with my Father!"

Jesus says you will be able to do the same and even greater "mighty miracles" than He did. That is not a small statement! After He died on the cross and was raised from the dead, He went to be with the Father, but He sent us the ultimate gift—the Holy Spirit.

> "But very truly I tell you, it is for your good
> that I am going away. Unless I go away, the
> Advocate [Holy Spirit] will not come to you;
> but if I go, I will send him to you."
> – John 16:7

While Jesus was on earth, He performed numerous miracles and taught many parables and lessons to crowds and individuals. He was close to the twelve disciples, who spent their days with Jesus teaching, leading, comforting, and guiding them. But when Jesus left earth, these things didn't stop or disappear. He didn't leave us hopeless and to fend for ourselves. He left us with the Holy Spirit.

As you read the verse below, try to take in the measure of power that the Holy Spirit offers. The same Spirit who could raise Jesus from the dead—so strong and undefeatable—can live in you too. Yes, our mortal bodies are alive, but we can have living mortal bodies and yet a dead spirit. Jesus wants you to have both.

> The Spirit of God, who raised Jesus from the
> dead, lives in you. And just as God raised
> Christ Jesus from the dead, he will give life to
> your mortal bodies by this same Spirit living
> within you.
> – Romans 8:11 (NLT)

So. . .
Invite Him in.
Become friends with Him.

Have conversations.

Speak and listen.

His voice, His power, and His wisdom are incomparable.

God's Heart to You

I can see your wheels spinning, trying to figure out your current situation. Confused and stressed about what decision to make or how to navigate this trial. I want to remind you that you don't have to figure anything out on your own. Take a moment to pause and listen to My Holy Spirit. I want to counsel you and guide you through this. You have analyzed every angle of this trial, trying to fight for breakthrough. But there are angles you haven't considered and crevices that only I know about, and I want to reveal them to you. Listen to My voice. I will give you the wisdom, discernment, and answers you are searching for.

Many moments throughout the day you feel powerless, not sure if you have the strength to continue on, the strength to do what you know is right or to say what needs to be said, the strength to step out in faith or help others in their distress. My Holy Spirit will empower you to do anything I call you to do. My strength will help you do the impossible. In fact, My strength is perfected in your weakness. You do not always have to be strong. My strength and power never weaken. Don't worry about your level of strength; just continue to trust and obey Me. Let Me be strong for you. Let Me empower you.

Stay close to Me. As you continue to connect with Me by speaking and listening, you will be transforming into someone more and more beautiful. Others will be drawn to you—and ultimately Me through you. You will have a newfound love for your neighbor. You will exude joy. You will have an internal peace and want to bring peace to disruptive situations. Your increased level of patience, kindness, and gentleness for not only others but for yourself will surprise you. You will actively fight for good. You will be faithful and consistent with your promises and with where I am calling you. You will have the self-control to say no to sin and yes to life-giving things. This is the fruit of staying in step with My Spirit.

With all the voices around you, My Holy Spirit will remind you what is true about your situation, about who you are and who I am. I will steady and realign your mind. I'll bring new life and hope to your sad and disappointed heart. I am for you in every way. I want to bless you and work with you to bless others.

Can I speak to you and guide you?

Can I do wonders in and through you?

Can I make you powerful and wise?

Can I make you powerful and wise?

☐ No, I'm not ready to engage with the Holy Spirit.

GOD: What reservations do you have about the Holy Spirit? I know many have seen Him as mysterious and are reluctant to connect with Him, so know that you are not alone if you think this. The Holy Spirit is for you. If you feel otherwise, please tell Me your thoughts.

☐ Yes, I am ready to hear from your Holy Spirit and for Him to do mighty things in and through me.

GOD: I am excited to share with you all that I am through My Holy Spirit. Transformation will start to happen in your mind and heart. As we build our relationship, you will see transformation in numerous other ways as well. Let Me show you...

7

Can I Give You a New Wardrobe?

What does your wardrobe look like these days? Are you pleased with what you see inside your closet? Do you like the shirts, pants, shoes, and jackets you put on each day? People's clothing can reflect their personality and show you a glimpse of who they are. In one person's closet you may see mainly neutral colors, and in another closet, bright and vibrant colors. You may see classy blouses, suits and ties, or vintage attire. We all have a wardrobe. Some have extravagant walk-in closets with name-brand clothing, and others just the bare necessities.

Countless magazine covers, billboards, and ads, as well as social media, influence how you perceive what is fashionable, trendy, and beautiful. There is great pressure to fit these molds and to feel accepted and celebrated. Regardless of what the world says is fashionable, there are styles you are naturally drawn to. As you walk down a street filled with people or browse the windows in a mall, some styles will stand out to you, and others will just blend in. Some you admire, and others not so much.

There's another wardrobe that doesn't get nearly as much attention, recognition, and chatter. It's less obvious at first glance. There's no "best dressed" award, billboard, or New York fashion week dedicated to highlight this kind of wardrobe. Not nearly as much time or money is invested to make needed improvements to this wardrobe. I would say this wardrobe is underrated, downplayed, and seen as secondary.

What wardrobe am I talking about?

The wardrobe of your soul.

Every morning you get dressed. You take off your pajamas and put on your shirt, pants, socks, shoes, watch, jewelry, makeup, and so on. This is never an option for you. You would never show up to work in your pajamas. Even when it's a casual day and you're only running errands, you'll at least put on some shoes and take a quick peek in the mirror to make sure you are not disheveled. You and I naturally want to present ourselves well to the world.

How often, would you say, do you take time to "dress" your soul?

Your soul represents your mind, will, and emotions. It's easy to "hide" these areas of life. The tendency is to put off addressing these parts or not give them the attention they deserve.

Mind: thoughts that go through your head and the things you meditate on.

Will: what you choose to do and refuse to do; the willful decisions you make.

Emotions: the feelings you experience (e.g., joy, excitement, anger, grief, confusion, etc.).

From the moment you wake up, your mind is thinking about all you must do that day. Your will is deciding to make breakfast, change clothes, and get in your car. Your emotions could be anything from excitement or dread for the day.

As important as it is to get physically dressed in the morning, it is just as, if not more, crucial to dress your soul. If you ignore your soul, you will be like a temperature gauge passively fluctuating with the good and the bad going on around you. If you're aware of and set your mind, will, and emotions to what is good and true, you will be like a thermostat that regulates the temperature in the room and those you come in contact with.

> *As important as it is to get physically dressed in the morning, it is just as, if not more, crucial to dress your soul.*

I'm sure you've had the experience of meeting someone you think is attractive but after a few minutes of conversation with that person, their appeal slowly slips away. Their anger, bitterness, and gossip repel you. You've likely had the opposite experience where you've met someone you're not initially attracted to, but their kindness, patience, listening ear, and encouragement make you want to spend additional time with them. In fact, they become more attractive by the minute, even though their outward appearance never changed.

Your soul shines through, whether or not you want it to. You can fake being happy or respectful to those around you, but if your soul is not doing well, it will soon show. It's exhausting pretending to be okay. I want to be whole inside. I want to genuinely be at peace, to be secure and content. I'm sure you do too.

You can't develop a healthy and whole soul on your own. Jesus and the Holy Spirit are kind and don't leave you in your current state. They desire to do the deepest and sweetest work to your soul. They go where few others are willing to go. No mess or turmoil scares them or is too hard to restore. Redemption is their specialty, stripping away the old and bringing in the new.

But you also have a role in your transformation. Your transformation is a partnership with Him. Just as you must intentionally take off and put on new clothes every day, the same is true with tending to your soul.

God says that to transform your mind, you need to renew it!

> Do not conform to the pattern of this world,
> but be transformed by the renewing of your
> mind. Then you will be able to test and approve
> what God's will is—his good, pleasing and
> perfect will.
> – Romans 12:2

You also need to remove certain thoughts and replace them with life-giving thoughts, like these:

> Whatever is true, whatever is noble, whatever
> is right, whatever is pure, whatever is lovely,

whatever is admirable—if anything is
excellent or praiseworthy—think about such
things.
– Philippians 4:8

Here God says how to clothe yourself in order to tend
to your will and emotions:

Therefore, as God's chosen people, holy and
dearly loved, clothe yourselves with compassion,
kindness, humility, gentleness and patience.
Bear with each other and forgive one another
if any of you has a grievance against someone.
Forgive as the Lord forgave you. And over all
these virtues put on love, which binds them all
together in perfect unity.
– Colossians 3:12–14

You are not clothing yourself in compassion, kindness,
humility, gentleness, and patience to be good enough, loved,
and chosen. You are already loved and chosen; there's nothing more to earn. You choose to clothe yourself in these
qualities because this is how He is clothed. You become a
reflection of Him. You become freer—
and more attractive! Who isn't drawn
to someone who is kind? And patient?

If your mind, will, and emotions
are healthy, your words and actions
will be too. Just as trees and plants
bear fruit, so does your soul. The fruit
of the Holy Spirit is love, joy, peace,

> *If your mind, will, and emotions are healthy, your words and actions will be too.*

patience, kindness, goodness, faithfulness, gentleness, and self-control, and these start internally, not externally. Trees and plants bear much fruit when they have rich soil and deep roots. Again, the origin of the fruit doesn't start at the tip of the branch but from deep within.

The Holy Spirit also gives you gifts—spiritual in nature—that bless you and the world around you. Just as fruit that comes from the Holy Spirit is part of our wardrobe, so are these spiritual gifts. They include:

- offering words of knowledge and wisdom for direction to others
- prophesying (giving encouragement) to someone
- faith, or the assurance that God will do what He has promised
- healings and miracles with the same power that raised Jesus from the dead
- the ability to discern between good and evil spirits
- speaking and/or interpreting tongues, a special and unique supernatural language given to you by the Holy Spirit

These are gifts that keep on giving, unlike that Christmas present you received five years ago that has now become irrelevant. These gifts change hearts and souls and produce exponential fruit.

The fruit and gifts of the Holy Spirit will set you apart. These are not only for your own good and edification, but they bless and bring life to a hurting and confused world. God will use and cultivate this fruit and these gifts in you as you live out the special plans He has prepared in advance for you.

There's one human race but many parts that make up that race. There's a temptation to become jealous and want to play someone else's role because it looks more glamorous or important. I encourage you to embrace and be confident in the part God is having *you* play. It's as significant and needed as all the other roles. When you think about a wardrobe, it doesn't contain only shirts or only pants. It consists of numerous items that make an outfit alluring, complete, and functional. Don't compete or try to conform to others. Stand in who and where God has placed you to be and what He has called *you* to do. This is where true influence and impact lie.

> *Stand in who and where God has placed you to be and what He has called you to do. This is where true influence and impact lie.*

What is the state of your soul (mind, will, and emotions)?

Pause for a few moments and take an inventory. So often we don't give ourselves the time and space to take note of the thoughts running through our minds, the default decisions we make, and to acknowledge the emotions we feel that are easy to just cover up so we can get to the end of the day. Break each one down. Then begin asking yourself a series of *why* questions to get to the root of your thinking, decisions, and feelings. Don't feel like you need to have this all figured out by the end of the day. It's a process. Be gracious to yourself because God is gracious toward you.

> *Be gracious to yourself because God is gracious toward you.*

When it comes to checking in with a friend, instead of asking, "How are you?" try asking, "How's your soul?" or "What have you been thinking about? What decision did you make about x, y, or z? How are you feeling?"

If you're wearing old mindsets and habits and haven't substituted for the new yet, what are you waiting for? Let God give you a makeover. Let the Holy Spirit bring to light how your soul is really doing. Let Him do some uprooting and transforming.

Once you start wearing your new wardrobe, you won't spend a second searching for the old one.

God's Heart to You

I have seen you critique yourself in the mirror, not liking what you were seeing, adjusting and tugging on your shirt and switching out your jeans, and not quite satisfied with your external self. Taking care of yourself is a good and noble thing, but I see the scales too often tipped toward putting most of your efforts on the outer, compared to the inner you.

I know it can be easy to be envious of your friends and neighbors, and I see the continuous pressure to look and act a certain way. Those voices are all around you and are hard to ignore.

Keeping up with the world's standard of beauty is costly in both time and money. But even more so, it's also costing you part of your identity. It's costing you an upgrade in your character and influence and what you can give to the world around you. Physical beauty is fleeting, but there are no bounds on how beautiful your soul can become.

I want to refresh your eyes to see yourself and people differently. I am a creative God and have made a spectrum of beauty that doesn't end. I want you to see people's hearts and souls like I do. I see their anxious minds. Do you? I see their good works, their pain, their potential. Do you?

I see you, too.

The world may applaud you one day, and the next, they may not even acknowledge you. But I don't leave you like that. I'm not fickle. I view beauty and success differently. Whether you are having a good or a bad hair day or your mind is taunting you, I'm here to stay.

Stay in tune with My Holy Spirit. Listen to His voice. He will tell you what is true about you. He will help you see more than the logo on someone's shirt or purse. He will do a new thing in you if you let Him. If you listen to Him, He will give you the words to speak to others that will go to their core.

Let go of the old lies you still believe.

Let go of the old decisions and habits you are making.

Let go of the depression, shame, and anxiety that have been toying with your emotions and weighing you down.

As you let go, replace it with what I say about you and the plans I have for you. Let Me create in you a new heart. Don't worry—you will still be you, just a more liberated and secure you.

Take all I have to offer. The fruit of My Holy Spirit. The gifts of My Holy Spirit. The calling I have placed in you.

The new is here and available for you.

Can I give you a new wardrobe?

Can I give you a new wardrobe?

☐ No, I LIKE THE WARDROBE I HAVE OR AM
   CONCERNED ABOUT HOW YOU MIGHT CHANGE
   ME.

GOD: What do you like most about your soul's
wardrobe right now? Are there any items in your soul's
closet that are old and worn, that need renewing or re-
placing? Let me know when you need help; I am here for
you.

☐ YES, I WANT A NEW WARDROBE! I WANT TO FULLY
   BE WHO YOU CREATED ME TO BE!

GOD: And the transformation continues! Thank
you for trusting Me with your mind, will, and emotions. As you trust Me with the transformation of your
soul, I have some adventures prepared for you. Are you
up for that?

8

Can I Take You on an Adventure?

Have you ever taken a road trip or hiked a long and winding trail you've never been on before? You were likely filled with excitement and anticipation, asking yourself, "What is it going to be like? Will the scenery be as beautiful as the pictures? Will it be as great as my friends and all the reviews say? Will it meet my expectations?" The destination is what we are enamored with and visualize in our minds. The goal is to get there, ideally quickly, and without too many interruptions.

But don't forget about what comes before the destination: the journey. The journey is not as easy to visualize. The destination has a picture attached to it, but the journey is often a blurry image, like when you're wearing eyeglasses with an expired prescription. You can make out a few objects close to you but are unable to see things in the distance. For your comfort and security, you want to know exactly what will happen and when, especially if you love to have a plan!

Sometimes your mind is so fixed on the destination that you can easily overlook or underestimate all that is happening along the way. The journey consists of roadblocks, detours, construction, little treasures, and unexpected surprises. Sometimes it goes faster than expected, and sometimes it's slower and likely full of interruptions and inconveniences. The challenges along the journey can cause you to wonder if you're headed in the right direction or if you should have ever left the starting gate in the first place.

One definition of *adventure* is "An unusual and exciting, typically hazardous, experience or activity."[2] Do you enjoy exploring unknown territory? Exploring is much more than pulling back the curtain and taking a peek. It's more than observing from a distance or from a bird's-eye view. Exploring is going through the unknown territory not knowing what may be around the corner. It takes a lot of courage to venture in a direction where you're not sure what's ahead or what you will find along the way. Or do you prefer to stay where it's familiar, where the territory is known and more predictable?

What is your default—the familiar or the unknown?

Life's middle name is *adventure*. Life doesn't always ask permission to stay where you are or move you into the unknown. Sometimes change happens to you without you wanting or asking for it. And other times you get to choose your adventures. You could read a hundred biographies that show the many adventures in a person's life, and they would all tell a different story. In each there are trials, triumphs,

---

[2] *Oxford English Dictionary*, s.v. "adventure," accessed October 11, 2020, https://www.lexico.com/en/definition/adventure.

unexpected twists and turns, and even some mundane moments, but every story is as unique as your fingerprints.

Take a moment to think about your life's story up until this point. What pictures or events come to mind? Which journeys and destinations would you like to go back to, and which ones do you wish never happened? Which journeys would you say you grew the most from? Whether you realize it or not, you are on a path to somewhere at this very moment.

Are you walking into the familiar or the unknown?

Do you like where you are headed?

How do you know if you should go to the right or the left, say yes or no, wait or go, hunker down or adventure out?

I cannot answer those questions for you, but the Holy Spirit probably has something to tell you about them. He knows how to direct you better than I do, and I'm certain there's a path for you, a race for you to run, a purpose wrapped around your everyday moments.

And what if I told you that you don't have to plan your future adventures by yourself, that there is someone who will walk with you into unknown territory and who you can trust to lead and guide you? God says He is your Shepherd. He is a master at leading you through unknown territory. The territory is unknown to you but not to Him. You don't know or see what is around the corner, but He does. You may often get scared or anxious, but He is steady. The

> *He is a master at leading you through unknown territory.*

valleys, obstacles, dangers, and enemies often deter you, but God cannot be deterred. That's why you and I need an all-wise and immovable Shepherd to help us choose to not stop at the edge of the unknown but to walk in and explore it.

> The LORD is my shepherd, I lack nothing.
> He makes me lie down in green pastures, he
> leads me beside quiet waters,
> he refreshes my soul. He guides me along the
> right paths for his name's sake.
> Even though I walk through the darkest
> valley, I will fear no evil, for you are with me;
> your rod and your staff, they comfort me.
> You prepare a table before me in the presence
> of my enemies.
> You anoint my head with oil;
> my cup overflows.
> Surely your goodness and love will follow me
> all the days of my life,
> and I will dwell in the house
> of the LORD forever.
> – Psalm 23:1–6

As you can see, in the midst of the unknown God provides leadership, rest, refreshment, guidance, comfort, protection, and favor. He reassures that His goodness and love will follow you. I don't know about you, but this is the reassurance I need to take confident steps into the unknown. Day by day, He leads. Day by day, He provides.

In our culture, the race that many are running is a race of to-do lists, never-ending competition with people they know and don't know, and seeing who can get to the finish line first! That's not how God intended us to run our races.

Running your race is doing the thing that God has called *you* to do—the gifts, passions, convictions, and personality He's instilled in you to work with. He has a mission for you. If you let Him be your Shepherd, He will protect you from going down the same rat race our culture is running, and lead you on a race designed and marked out specifically for you. It's not a race of obligation, striving, and competition, but one of trust, obedience, faith, and joy. Your race will look different from the next person, and that is more than okay. It's beautiful and thrilling. In fact, at this moment, He's writing a story tailor-made for you and Him to run together.

> *It's not a race of obligation, striving, and competition, but one of trust, obedience, faith, and joy.*

God walked many people in the Bible through some wild and unique adventures:

- Noah building an ark (the first boat ever made), and he and his family surviving a worldwide flood (Genesis 6–9)
- the Israelites, while chased by the Egyptians, being led to safety by God parting the Red Sea (Exodus 14)
- the walls of Jericho falling down after Joshua and the Israelites marched around it for seven days at the command of God (Joshua 6)
- David, as just a young man, defeating Goliath with a sling and stone (1 Samuel 17)
- Shadrach, Meshach, and Abednego being thrown into a furnace, Jesus appearing in the fire with them, and all escaping without a hair being singed (Daniel 3)
- Daniel being thrown into the lions' den, coming out without a scratch (Daniel 6)

- Peter walking on water (Matthew 14:22–33)
- Jesus putting mud on a blind man's eyes, healing him (John 9:1–12)
- the creation of the church and people first being baptized in the Holy Spirit (Acts 2)

These are just a few. Each of the above stories are examples of significant moments in their lives. However, many events took place before and after those "big" moments too. There was a journey that led up to those destinations and journeys that followed. Even though these adventures happened during biblical times, God is still orchestrating big and small adventures every day. The adventures haven't stopped, even if they have appeared to. He may be taking you on an adventure, and you may not even realize you are right in the middle of it.

To adventure with God and run your race with perseverance, you need to lay down things that are holding you back, the sin that keeps you from running freely, and fix your eyes ahead and not in the past. You must have an open heart to what He is calling you to do and be willing to do what is illogical and outside the norm.

Jesus's race took Him to the cross. What propelled Him toward this act was the joy in what would be accomplished, obedience to His heavenly Father, and His fiery love for you. As you learned earlier, His death didn't end in death but in defeating death and rising again. He calls you to remember this so that you don't lose heart or faith as you run the race He has called you to endure whatever pain and praise that may come alongside on this adventure.

Therefore, since we are surrounded by such
a great cloud of witnesses, let us throw off
everything that hinders and the sin that
so easily entangles. And let us run with
perseverance the race marked out for us,
fixing our eyes on Jesus, the pioneer and
perfecter of faith. For the joy set before him
he endured the cross, scorning its shame,
and sat down at the right hand of the throne
of God. Consider him who endured such
opposition from sinners, so that you will not
grow weary and lose heart.
– Hebrews 12:1–3

Life with God is not boring or insignificant. When you try to control
everything or live in fear, it makes life
burdensome. When you surrender to

> *Life with God is not boring or insignificant.*

what God wants for your life and say yes to adventure, I believe He will introduce you to people you would never have
met, places you would never have gone to, and adventures
you would have missed out on. A yes to His ways is so much
better than a yes to our ways.

He will not lay out every detail for you. He will not tell
you exactly what will happen one year from now. He asks
you to trust Him. Humans want to see and know what is
around every corner, what will happen next. Even the most
spontaneous of people like to plan and prepare to some degree. If you only rely on what you know, what you can see,
and what makes sense to you, you will miss out on the new
things He wants to bring your way.

Trust in the LORD with all your heart
and lean not on your own understanding;
in all your ways submit to him,
and he will make your paths straight.
  – Proverbs 3:5–6

Trust > Understanding.

God calls you to walk by faith and not by sight. He calls you to this because it's easy to be deceived by what you "see." A challenging situation or circumstance might appear like everything is falling apart, when really God may be doing some rearranging and making room for new things in your life. No one enjoys trials, but this is where most of our character building happens.

> *Trust >*
> *Understanding*

Consider it pure joy, my brothers and sisters,
whenever you face trials of many kinds,
because you know that the testing of your
faith produces perseverance. Let perseverance
finish its work so that you may be mature
and complete, not lacking anything.
– James 1:2–4

For our light and momentary troubles are
achieving for us an eternal glory that far
outweighs them all. So we fix our eyes not
on what is seen, but on what is unseen, since
what is seen is temporary, but what is unseen
is eternal.
– 2 Corinthians 4:17–18

The adventure ahead and all that it entails will require trust and faith in Him. It will require letting go of some of your expectations of how you think things should go. It will require embracing the unknown. This adventure is meant for your good, to refine you and give you ample opportunities to love and serve others.

Are you willing to stop trusting your sight and start trusting His hand?

Do you trust His love and care for you?

Are you ready to experience all He has in store for you?

Faith > fear

His plan > your plan

The journey may be hard and the adventure risky, but what do you say? Are you in?

If yes, here's a simple declaration:

> *All I need I have. It's You and me.*
> *There's immeasurably more. Let's go!*

God's Heart to You

I see your frustration, fear, and wanting to figure things out, and know how the story will end. From your perspective, things in your life look like they've come to a dead end, things look so messy and out of control. Even though things appear bleak, I have not left you to walk this road alone. From My perspective, I see opportunity and new beginnings. Lift your head. Take your gaze off your situation, problems, and trials, and look at Me. I want to replenish you and renew your hope. This journey without Me will lead to striving and hanging on with white knuckles. It will be fruitless. I don't want that for you. I have so much for you in this season.

I want to be your Shepherd in this journey. I want to show you things you haven't seen before. I want to be your daily provision. I want to show you something new and take you to places you have not been before, both in physical territory and in your heart and mind. You will begin to have a new perspective about this race I have you on, and fear will slowly leave as anticipation floods in.

As you walk into unknown territory, do not be afraid. All the unknowns you are experiencing are not unknown to Me. I see. I know. Walk by faith, trusting My hand and My heart. I am for you.

Your story is in process, and I am writing every page of it. This adventure is one for the books. Your story is not only for you but also for those around you, to spread hope and to let others know I am with them too.

I invite you to take My hand.

Come.

Let's go.

Can I take you on an adventure?

Can I take you on an adventure?

☐ No, I'm not ready for the unknown. It
scares me, and I want to sit in the familiar
a little longer.

GOD: I understand. The unknown and walking by
faith is uncomfortable. It is risky. Do you trust My love
and care for you? Do you trust I have good things ahead
for you? If not, why not? Tell Me your reservations.

☐ Yes, Here we go, God, I'm ready to follow
you on an adventure!

GOD: There are so many places and experiences I'm
excited to show you and take you through. This is just
the beginning. Keep holding My hand and trusting
Me. And rest assured that even though some of these
adventures will include trials, I will fight for you each
step of the way.

9

Can I Fight for You?

At least once if not numerous times throughout your life, you've either observed or been part of a fight. It may have been physical or verbal, but there have been times you've battled it out with someone. Kids and siblings do it all the time. Politicians do it, just in a more "grown-up" way. Co-workers, competitors, athletes, animals, and people on TV fight on a daily basis. Fights can be pretty ugly and not the most pleasant thing to watch or be a part of. You may have the urge to step in and break up the fight, while other times you retreat to safety.

After a fight you may have realized you were in the wrong and crossed the line in something you said or did or in your attitude. Other times you were sincerely fighting for what was good and right. Your motivations were on point, and you only wanted to protect, defend, or progress a cause.

Has there ever been a time when you were fighting a battle on your own? Do you wish someone had come to your rescue and taken you to safety where it was calm and peaceful? Where you didn't have to fight anymore but could rest and have someone else take the blows for you?

That battle may be depression or an anxiety attack. It may be a bully at home, at school, or in the workplace who tries to make you feel small with their words. You might be battling for breakthrough in your life, to defeat that addiction, to finally be married, to save your marriage, to get out of debt, or to be healed from your chronic illness. Maybe you're battling the giant of fear, and it's stopping you in your tracks and keeping you from your dreams.

What battles are you fighting right now?

What areas of life do you feel pushback and are struggling to advance in?

Take inventory of these battles. Name them. Call them out. Look each one in the eye.

Now what? You're courageously looking your battle in the eye, a battle that has been going on for far too many rounds. What is your battle strategy? Battles require a strategy for defeat; do you have one? You can keep throwing punches for the rest of your days, but it may only result in you becoming utterly exhausted and even nearing the point of surrender.

What is your battle strategy?

A boy named David in the Bible had a battle plan. A serious face-off was about to ensue between the Philistines and the Israelites. The Philistines had a giant named Goliath who was more than ready to battle it out with anyone willing to step up to the plate. The stakes were high. The nation of the loser of this battle had to submit to the other side. Second place was not an option here. There were no do-overs, no plan B. Winning the first round was essential.

Many Israelites were fearful of taking on the challenge of standing up against the Philistine warrior.

David, small in stature and young in age, approached the scene and offered to fight this crucial battle. He wasn't afraid to look Goliath in the eye. Many dismissed him as only a boy. But David not only had experience fighting off predators in the fields while protecting his sheep but he also had an unwavering confidence in the Lord. He knew how the Lord had made and prepared him. He was firm in his identity.

King Saul put armor on David that was traditionally used for battle, but David was not accustomed to this armor and it was too heavy for him, so it was more of a hindrance than a help. Instead, he used stones and a sling. This strategy was not found in any battle-plan manual and was seen as foolish and immature by his enemy. But that had no effect on David's confidence. Goliath's words did not intimidate or sway him.

> David said to the Philistine, "You come against me with sword and spear and javelin, but I come against you in the name of the LORD Almighty. . . . All those gathered here will know that it is not by sword or spear that the Lord saves; for the battle is the LORD's, and he will give all of you into our hands." As the Philistine moved closer to attack him, David ran quickly toward the battle line to meet him.
> – 1 Samuel 17:45, 47–48

Goliath was defeated that day—not partially but fully.

Catch that—the battle is the Lord's! These battles do not belong to you. They are not yours to win. And because the battle is the Lord's, you can run quickly to the battle line with confidence and vigor. Maybe you feel defeated and exhausted because you've been fighting in your own strength and strategies, and the armor others suggested you wear is only weighing you down. It's tempting to fight how the "elite" and "experienced" tell you to fight. If David had done this, he would have lost. Fight your battles with God's guidance and not what others perceive to be the best method or plan. It may look different than how the last person fought a similar fight or even how you won your last battle, but fight with full confidence that the Lord will come through for you again.

> *Because the battle is the Lord's, you can run quickly to the battle line with confidence and vigor.*

Your eyes have a certain perception of what battles entail. God speaks of your struggles in this way:

> For our struggle is not against flesh and
> blood, but against the rulers, against the
> authorities, against the powers of this dark
> world and against the spiritual forces of evil
> in the heavenly realms.
> – Ephesians 6:12

I don't know about you, but I don't want to fight the spiritual forces of evil on my own. That's far beyond my ability and pay grade. Thank goodness God has not left us to defend ourselves. In fact, He gave us a set of armor that works. Not the type of armor that Saul suggested, but the type David tapped into:

> Finally, be strong in the Lord and in his mighty power. Put on the full armor of God, so that you can take your stand against the devil's schemes. . . . Therefore put on the full armor of God, so that when the day of evil comes, you may be able to stand your ground, and after you have done everything, to stand. Stand firm then, with the belt of truth buckled around your waist, with the breastplate of righteousness in place, and with your feet fitted with the readiness that comes from the gospel of peace. In addition to all this, take up the shield of faith, with which you can extinguish all the flaming arrows of the evil one. Take the helmet of salvation and the sword of the Spirit, which is the word of God.
> – Ephesians 6:10–11, 13–17

Put on the full armor of God:

Belt of Truth:
- supports the core and other pieces of armor; a stabilizer that allows you to move and live freely
- fights against Satan's deceptions, lies, and illusions

- allows you to believe the things God has spoken and taught you in the Bible and through His Holy Spirit

Breastplate of Righteousness:

- protects the heart—your thoughts, feelings, will, and conscience
- fights against Satan distorting, redirecting, tampering, and influencing your heart
- allows you to love the things God loves and hate the things God hates, aligning your life to walk in the truth

Gospel of Peace:

- moves you forward with the feet of readiness
- fights against Satan's attempt to add confusion, turmoil, anxiety, and internal discord to your life
- allows you to receive peace from Him and give it out in return

Shield of Faith:

- instills the confidence to walk into what God is calling you to do
- fights against Satan's flaming arrows of lies and the distractions that stop faith in its tracks
- allows you to express your faith through action

Helmet of Salvation:

- protects the mind so it can be effective
- fights against destructive thoughts in your mind
- allows you to have a healthy mind and fix your thoughts on what is true and lovely

Sword of the Spirit:

- is God's word, which destroys lies that come at you
- fights against lies that Satan wants to tell you about yourself and God's character

- allows you to have confidence in the promises and truths He has spoken to you

These are not passive pieces of armor. They are not elective or ordered a la carte. Each of these six pieces of armor are used in unison to actively protect and fight on your behalf. You just need to put them on. And as you do, He says, "Be still, and know that I am God" (Psalm 46:10). "Be still" doesn't necessarily mean *do nothing* but, rather, *stop striving* in your own strength and let God unleash His power on your behalf.

God doesn't *have* to fight for you— He wants to. He is your Defender. Psalm 91 describes His fierce love and strength for you:

> *God doesn't have to fight for you—He wants to.*

Whoever dwells in the shelter of the Most High
will rest in the shadow of the Almighty.
I will say of the LORD, "He is my refuge and my
fortress, my God, in whom I trust."
Surely he will save you from the fowler's snare
and from the deadly pestilence.
He will cover you with his feathers, and under
his wings you will find refuge; his faithfulness
will be your shield and rampart.
You will not fear the terror of night, nor the
arrow that flies by day,

nor the pestilence that stalks in the darkness,
nor the plague that destroys at midday.
A thousand may fall at your side,
ten thousand at your right hand,
but it will not come near you.
You will only observe with your eyes
and see the punishment of the wicked.
 If you say, "The LORD is my refuge,"
and you make the Most High your dwelling,
no harm will overtake you,
no disaster will come near your tent.
For he will command his angels concerning you
to guard you in all your ways;
they will lift you up in their hands,
so that you will not strike your foot against a
stone.
You will tread on the lion and the cobra;
you will trample the great lion and the serpent.
"Because he loves me," says the LORD, "I will
rescue him;
 I will protect him, for he acknowledges my
name.
He will call on me, and I will answer him;
I will be with him in trouble,
I will deliver him and honor him.
With long life I will satisfy him
and show him my salvation."

Put on His armor.
Be still as you call on Him.
Put your confidence in His strength.

Trust in His faithfulness.
The battle is the Lord's.
Know, in advance, that you have already won.

God's Heart to You

I know it's been a long haul for you. You have been relentlessly fighting battles that are draining you. It appears they will never end or that they might just defeat you one day. I see you struggling, striving, wrestling—and tired. These battles you're facing are too strong for you. I see them overwhelming and overtaking you. Your feet are dragging, and your heart is heavy.

But this doesn't have to be. Battles are not meant to be fought on your own. I want to fight for you. Put off all the armor the world has given you and told you would work. Surrender your battle plan; I want to give you a new way to fight. My plan includes confidence, reassurance, rest, and victory.

But for Me to do so . . .

Can you lay down the lies this battle has caused you to believe and put on what I have been saying is true?

Can you lay down the unrighteousness and wrong-doing your battle has tempted you with and put on what is righteous and good?

Can you lay down the strife and unrest this battle brings and put on the act of pursuing peace?

Can you lay down the doubt this battle has filled you with and put on faith, and trust that I'm working?

Can you lay down the forgetfulness of your salvation and inheritance this battle has distracted you with and put on the security you have in Me?

Can you lay down the pride of fighting lies on your own that this battle has brought and put on the confidence of the Spirit's power and protection?

This exchange of laying down and putting on will secure a win for the battle you're facing. I know it's not your natural way of fighting, but I can tell you that you'll be glad you did. Trust that I am fighting for you. Nothing can prevail against Me.

I am for you and not against you.

Can I be your hero?

Can I fight for you?

Response to God's invitation

Can I fight for you?

☐ No, I am unsure that You will come through for me. This battle is overwhelming, and I can't imagine it being defeated.

GOD: I am ready to fight for you at any time. Nothing is too hard for Me. What have you been fighting for a long time that seems insurmountable?

☐ Yes, I'm tired. I need You to fight my battles.

GOD: Dear one, I am and will continue to fight for you. I fight your battles and will carry your burdens. I love you.

10

Can I Carry That for You?

Have you ever felt like the weight of the world is on your shoulders? Your checklist is long, the demands are great, and the load feels forever heavy. You continue to encourage yourself to keep trudging through work, home life, relationships, and everything else along your path. You start to wonder if it will always be this way. You think, *Maybe this is just how life is. Just keep plowing forward no matter how tired you are. Fatigue and burnout are badges of honor, right?* Not quite. Yet this is what the world says. If you're not in a million activities, getting ahead, and exhausted at the end of the day, you didn't do enough, says our culture.

You carry many things throughout your day. From housework, yard work, taking care of family members, and running to and from errands, your body can be physically pushed to the limits. You also carry a lot in your mind and heart. Fear, worries, and anxieties are just a few that continually want your attention and consume your mental energy.

Often the weight of what you carry is disguised in "caring" about something or someone. Worry often dresses up as caring so it can be invited to the party. However, worry has no productivity attached to it, like a hamster wheel you

> *Worry often dresses up as caring so it can be invited to the party.*

put yourself on that can literally make you sick. Caring turns into worry when you start to spin your wheels and fret over things you can't control. You think, *If I'm not stressing about this thing, then I don't care enough. You have to stress to care about others or your own situation, right?* Wrong. Would you want someone who is full of worry to come to your aid? Or someone who is clearheaded, positive, and steady and who offers constructive advice to help you move forward? When a person cares, they don't control but instead listen, intentionally follow up, and actively find ways to assist you.

God says numerous times to not worry or be anxious because He cares for you.

> *He doesn't stress about you. He cares for you.*

He doesn't worry about you.
He doesn't stress about you.
He cares for you.

> Cast all your anxiety on him because he cares
> for you.
> –1 Peter 5:7

The word *cast* means to "throw something forcefully in a specified direction." [3] And in what direction are you to

---

[3] *Oxford English Dictionary*, s.v. "cast," accessed October 6, 2020, https://www.lexico.com/definition/cast.

throw your anxiety? On Him. Most people don't volunteer for others to throw their anxieties on them. The goal is to get rid of anxieties, not add more. He wouldn't offer this invitation if He couldn't handle it. Your anxieties are a burden to you, but they're not a burden to Him. It's all because He "cares for you." *Care* means to "attach importance, to look after, and to provide for the needs of." [4]

When you throw your anxieties, burdens, and worries on Him, they don't just passively sit on His lap. He is actively attending to the things that concern you. But you need to throw them from your hands into His hands. Cut the cord. They leave you and are no longer attached. Many follow their anxieties around like their worry is in charge and they are at its beck and call. And remember, if you've cast your anxiety but somehow find yourself holding it again, you can always give it back.

Not only does God say to cast your anxieties on Him but to also pray and express thanksgiving to release the burdens you're carrying. This results in a peace where He is continually guarding your heart and mind.

It's like a math equation.

Anxiety + casting + praying + thanksgiving = peace and protection

> Do not be anxious about anything, but in
> every situation, by prayer and petition, with
> thanksgiving, present your requests to God.
> And the peace of God, which transcends all

[4] *Oxford English Dictionary*, s.v. "care," accessed October 6, 2020, https://www.lexico.com/definition/care.

understanding, will guard your hearts and your
minds in Christ Jesus.
– Philippians 4:6–7

Worry does not add life; it distracts from living a life of
peace and fulfillment.

Who of you by being worried can add a
single day to his life's span?
– Matthew 6:27 (NASB)

We are responsible for today, not tomorrow.

"Refuse to worry about tomorrow, but deal
with each challenge that comes your way,
one day at a time. Tomorrow will take care of
itself."
– Matthew 6:34 (TPT)

What is that one thing that feels so heavy in your heart
right now? Financial troubles? A pending divorce? The loss
of a loved one? Regret and shame over past decisions? Lone-
liness? Unforgiveness? Fear of an unknown future? Nervous-
ness about an upcoming meeting or business deal? A bad
health report? Sometimes these things simply feel unbearable. You think about the situation nearly all day, every day.
You take a deep sigh and ask, "Will this ever pass?"

You and I are called to bear each other's burdens.

Carry each other's burdens, and in this way
you will fulfill the law of Christ.
– Galatians 6:2

Close, intimate friendships are paramount when walking through this life. We can share, relate, comfort, encourage, and sacrifice for one another. But what happens when your friends are not in sight or their words fall short of the comfort you desperately need? Then what? Do you need to take over from there? No. This is where the Holy Spirit, your Counselor, steps in and says what your heart needs to hear. The perfect words. Since He knows your heart and is perfectly wise, He can speak into those deep trenches where there's no light and no words to describe how you're feeling.

He not only wants to speak to you but take your burdens from you too. That "thing"—whatever it is—may still be there, but the weight of it is no longer yours to carry because it's His now. Do you remember when He carried the weight of the cross? The weight of every sin that was committed as well as all future sins? Remember how He handled that weight? He fully carried it, defeated it, and rose from the dead. He is alive today. He was and is victorious. If He can handle that unbearable weight, He can handle the heaviest of burdens you carry. When your problem increases in size, so does the cross. The size of your problem is never too big for the cross to overcome.

He's not just another helpful person—He is God. He is able to take care of the messiest and scariest situations. If you release that burden and hand it over to Him, He can do more with it than you can. Release it. Cast it—again and again if you need to. Let Him revive and redeem it. The results are His. He cares.

> *He's not just another helpful person— He is God.*

Can I Be Your God?

"Come to me, all you who are weary and
burdened, and I will give you rest.
Take my yoke upon you and learn from me,
for I am gentle and humble in heart, and you
will find rest for your souls. For my yoke is easy
and my burden is light."
   – Matthew 11:28–30

You may have grown up thinking that God is continually pointing His finger at you, calling out all your wrongs and how you have fallen short, and that you need to fix your own messes. You may have thought you should walk around feeling burdened because that is the repercussion of your wrongs and others' wrongs to you. Yes, you need to play a part too—asking for forgiveness, forgiving others, reconciliation, turning away from bad habits and sins—but Jesus came to take these burdens from you, and it would be a disservice to His death on the cross if you held on to them. He wants to give you rest. He is gentle and humble in heart. He's a safe place to disclose your hardships and heartaches and a soft place to land.

Cast your anxiety on Him.

Watch Him work.

Let go, and enjoy resting for a change.

God's Heart to You

I see your pace. You're busy running and achieving. People around you see you are advancing. But I see something different. I see rounded shoulders, tired eyes, the stomachache, and the heavy heart. The pace of life on the outside isn't matching the pace of life on the inside, and I see both clearly.

These burdens you've been carrying and managing have taken a toll on you. I see when your heart drops and your thoughts race. I see the nagging discouragement you feel and the temptation to retreat. I see.

This is not the life I intended for you. Yes, I said that in this world you will have trouble. But I also said, "Take heart, I have overcome the world!" I live in you, and I am greater than any person in the world, including my enemy, Satan. I desire for you to walk lightly and freely. Trials were not meant to weigh you down or defeat you. Trials and joy were meant to walk hand in hand. I have a different plan for your trials, troubles, and burdens. Satan would love to use them to weigh you down to the point of losing all hope and make you ineffective. I make use of these trials. Not only will trials not defeat you but they will advance you! They will create in you a level of perseverance you never had before. The end result of these trials will make you complete, mature, not lacking anything.

Tell me what is burdening you. You can be honest with Me. No news you tell Me will shake or disturb Me. As your Father, even though I can see what is burdening you, I want to hear from you how these burdens are affecting your heart.

Will you allow Me to carry your pain so it won't overwhelm and overtake you? Your pain doesn't stop or slow down the work I want to do in your life. I can be trusted to sustain you through your pain. If you invite Me into your pain and burdens, and not try to manage them on your own, I will do something special with them. I will counsel you through this challenging time. My strong right hand will shape this trial into something

that will result in good. Can you do something you

haven't done in a long time? Can you loosen your

grip and control on this thing that is weighing you

down? You don't have to manage or figure it out on

your own. Pray and lift up your requests to Me. Choose

thanksgiving; it will bring clarity to what I'm doing

during this time.

Will you throw your anxiety on Me?

Can I carry that for you?

Can I carry that for you?

☐ No, I'm not ready to give what I've been carrying over to You. I think I can control and handle this for a while longer.

GOD: What are you currently carrying? What are you doing with the thing you are carrying? What about My ability to carry this burden do you doubt?

☐ Yes, please take this heavy burden I am carrying. I'm ready to let go of it.

GOD: Wonderful. I am happy and able to carry it for you and start resolving this burden and trial for your benefit. You will soon feel lighter and freer. I know waiting can also feel like a burden at times—I'd love to carry you through that as well.

11

Can I Stand in Line with You?

If there is one thing in this world that is pretty much universally unwelcomed and seldom enjoyed, it is waiting. I've never heard anyone say, "I wish this line was a little longer so I could spend more of my day standing here waiting," "I hope my dreams take a little longer to come to pass," or "I hope this cold or sickness sticks around; I want to wait another month for my healing."

In a situation where you must wait or are unable to speed up the process, frustration comes. Something inside you gets unsettled and restless. You get antsy. You don't understand why this thing is taking longer than you think it should. It's easy to believe that if it happened on the timeline you created in your mind, then all the stars would align, everything would be in order, and your world would proceed to go smoothly without any bumps or hiccups. But you and I know life has plenty of bumps and hiccups. Yet secretly, we continue to strive to have as smooth and comfortable a ride as possible.

Waiting can be excruciating at times. As the waiting period in your life progresses, you may start to ask questions such as:

- What is the purpose of this waiting?
- Should I stop hoping in the thing I'm waiting for?
- When will this be over?
- When will it come?
- Should I take matters into my own hands to speed up the process?

When circumstances are not lining up and life is still not making sense, it's easy to let your view of God's character and goodness become cloudy. You may start asking additional questions such as:

- Have You forgotten about me, God? Do you see me?
- Will You come through for me?
- Are You withholding from me?
- God, have You abandoned me?
- If You're a good God, why would You make me wait this long?

Over time, as these questions persist without many answers and the doubt begins to weigh on you, you come to believe things about waiting that simply aren't true. Without a healthy perspective on the purpose of waiting, the frustration and doubt only continue to fester. So, it's imperative to remember what is true about waiting and why it is not only good but necessary at times.

Here are just a few examples of the lies and truths about waiting:

Lie #1: Waiting is a loss.

You may tend to believe that fast progression equals bigger, better, and best. More gets done. And the more that gets done, the more you can progress and move forward in life. You see waiting as just slowing you down and getting you behind. Behind what? Behind the expectations you have for your life, expectations of "I thought that would happen by now. This is not how I pictured things going. My reality is not matching up to what I had imagined my timeline to be." You see your expectations not being met and the rest of the world steaming full speed ahead. And if you "fall behind," then a sense of failure rests on you.

Truth: Waiting is gain.

Even though waiting can be painful, it can remind you that you are not in control of most things, and it forces you to lean into God's timing and trust that He is who He says He is. In the process of waiting, you *gain* perseverance, trust, patience, and an intimacy with God. These are traits you need in every area of life, for the rest of your life. It can also be a gift when you don't get what you want when you want it, because often there's a better thing in store for you. You never would have received it if your first request were granted. You gained something better in the end.

> *In the process of waiting, you gain perseverance, trust, patience, and an intimacy with God.*

Lie #2: Waiting is a blank space.

When the future is unclear, you begin to believe your story has been paused and the pages have stopped turning. You can't handle the idea of nothing happening. When there's a sense that nothing is happening, something rises up in you to want to make something happen, to fill in the gaps, and to take the pen and start writing your own story. Your view is incredibly limited, simply because of your humanity. You can only partially see what is happening in your immediate circle and in the present hour. You can only plan days or weeks into the future, and even then, half those things may never happen due to ever-changing circumstances that are out of your control. You and I love certainty, and it's naturally frustrating when things seem to be at a standstill. But despite appearances, the "blank space" is only an illusion.

Truth: Waiting is filled with action.

Waiting is not a black hole of nothingness. In fact, there is so much happening your eyes can't see and your ears can't hear. Things are happening. Things are moving. There is a trust and belief that comes into play here. Just because you can't see anything happening doesn't mean that your world has stopped. The thing you want to come about often doesn't plop down in front of you. It appears through a "process." Take heart, God never stops working. And remember, you are still on assignment.

> *Take heart, God never stops working.*

Lie #3: Waiting periods should be sped up.

Since waiting is rarely ideal, there's a temptation to want to lessen or decrease the waiting period. The length of the waiting period is unknown. Will you have to wait a few more hours, a couple more days, weeks, till the end of the year, or a decade? You think, *There's no way I'm going to wait weeks, let alone years! I'm going to find a way to speed this process up.* So, you look around every corner, come up with new strategies, network, advertise your need, and strive with everything in you to move things along. The belief that a shorter waiting period is better or equals less pain is false. If you get what you're not ready for or what is not meant for you, it can result in more heartache than the pain of waiting a little longer.

Truth: Waiting periods are intentional.

> *Waiting periods were built into the framework of life. They're not accidental.*

Waiting periods were built into the framework of life. They're not accidental. You've been in waiting periods your whole life, starting in your mother's womb. You and your mother had to wait nine months for you to arrive in this world. This waiting period was crucial to allow you time to grow and develop and for your mother to have time to prepare all the things you would need when you came. This concept of preparation applies to numerous other areas of life as well, like a pre-game warm-up. You could just jump into the game, but the warm-up will make you readier for what the game will bring.

Lie #4: Waiting is depressing.

When you desire something and it hasn't arrived yet, it can be discouraging, disheartening, and disappointing and can even lead to depression. You think, *How can I be happy when I have this ache in my heart? I will be happy when that thing arrives.* Even though these feelings are real and often valid, they are not meant to define and control this season.

Life hasn't stopped. God's assignment for you is laced with grace, peace, and hope.

Truth: Waiting brings strength.

God is able to do a refinement in you with the tool of waiting like almost nothing else can. It builds your trust, your faith, and your dependence on Him. Why does that matter? You will have gained the gift of perseverance that will equip you in future waiting periods and trials, because they will come. And when they come, you won't be overcome. When the thing you're waiting for hasn't come, it leaves an open space for other things God wants you to focus on. It can lead to advancement in other areas of your life. Don't let what's missing overshadow all the other amazing opportunities and blessings in your life that are happening now. The beautiful thing is that when you wait with and on God, you *gain*!

> Even youths grow tired and weary,
> and young men stumble and fall.
> But those who wait upon the LORD, will
> renew their strength;
> they will mount up with wings like eagles;
> they will run and not grow weary,
> they will walk and not faint.
> – Isaiah 40:30–31 (BSB)

As you navigate through the truths and lies about waiting, it's okay if you still do not understand all that God is doing. In fact, He says that often you won't because His thoughts and actions are above what you would often choose:

For My thoughts are not your thoughts,
neither are your ways my ways, declares the
Lord.
For as the heavens are higher than the earth,
so are my ways higher than your ways
and my thoughts than your thoughts.
– Isaiah 55:8–9 (ESV)

Over and over He says to *trust* in Him. To call on Him.
To look to Him.

I lift up my eyes up to the mountains—
where does my help come from?
My help comes from the Lord,
the Maker of heaven and earth.
– Psalm 121:1–2

Don't just wait out the waiting. How you react to waiting will determine what this season will look like for you.

Waiting it out leads to:	Waiting on God leads to:
despair	renewed strength
striving to make things happen	experiencing His peace and provision
doubt	increased trust
survival mode	growth, advancement
hopelessness	hopeful expectation, anticipation for the future
inactivity, standstill	walking by faith, boldly following the Holy Spirit's lead

> *Waiting reveals what our prize is.*

Waiting reveals what our prize is. Is it Him, or is it that thing you're waiting for? What do you long for more? What will be the state of your heart if that thing never comes? What if He were all you had? What if you gained nothing else from this world? What if He didn't give you the thing you were waiting for but instead gave you something you didn't know existed and filled those longings with better things than your initial yearnings? What if He gave you more than you asked for but you had to walk through the wilderness of waiting to get there? What if He built a level of perseverance and character in you that prepared and developed you in a way you couldn't have achieved on your own?

> *Waiting is one of the most underrated gifts given to us by God.*

Waiting is one of the most underrated gifts given to us by God. It is one of the things that comes with life that none of us wants but our character depends on it. Our future depends on it.

Take heart—He never stops working on your behalf.

Waiting is not loss; it's gain.

Waiting on Him leads to renewed strength.

So, what are you waiting for? Are you ready and willing to take a second look at what God is doing in this season, and wait well?

God's Heart to You

I know it's hard to understand why you've been waiting so long. I feel your ache and see your longings. I see your frustrations and hear your questions. I know doubt has crept in and is battling your faith.

It may not look like anything is happening. Yet I didn't call you to trust your eyes but to walk by faith and to trust My faithful hand, to trust that I am working on your behalf. Even in this very moment I am orchestrating future events, conversations, and relationships. You do not foresee these things; they are incomprehensible to you. I don't expect you to "perform" to make these things happen in your own effort. Just stay in tune with My voice. Follow My promptings. I will do the heavy lifting. I will make the impossible happen.

In this unknown season, cast your anxiety and fear on Me. Your worry doesn't solve this situation; it only steals your peace. I want to remind you of who I am to you during this season of waiting. I want to reaffirm that My eyes have not left you and I have not forgotten you. I don't change like shifting shadows. I'm not here for you one day and the next day gone.

I keep My promises to you. I will never leave nor forsake you. I won't leave you dry and empty. I will satisfy and provide. You can bank on who I am; I will not fail you.

Trust in Me for I am bringing more. It's coming.

You don't have to wait alone.

Can I stand in line with you?

Can I stand in line with you?

☐ No, I don't think I can wait any longer. I
feel the need to proceed and find a way to
make my desires happen on my own.

GOD: I know you have been experiencing a lot of
pain while waiting. What has been the most painful
part about waiting for you? Do you feel like your hope
and strength have left you? I want to remind you that
I have not left you in this waiting season. And I want
to gently caution you to not take matters into your
own hands as it may forfeit something special I have in
store for you. As you wait a little longer, let's continue
to dialogue about this.

❑ YES, THANK YOU FOR STANDING IN LINE WITH
ME AND HELPING ME PERSEVERE THROUGH THIS
WAITING SEASON.

GOD: I am doing wonders in your waiting. They
will be revealed to you in time. Thank you for trusting
Me. I am about to knock your socks off with the sweet
unexpected.

12

Can I Knock Your Socks Off?

"Impossible."

"That will never happen."

"I'm not sure that dream will ever come to pass."

"I can't imagine being debt free."

"I can't imagine being healed from this disease."

"I'm not sure my joy will ever come back."

"It's a lost cause."

"There's no hope left in this situation."

Have you ever thought or said any of these statements? Most people have. It's understandable—some situations are hard to imagine ever changing or getting better, and it simply feels impossible.

When things look hopeless, it's easy to give up and dismiss the chance for a better outcome. Expectations for improvement decrease with each passing day. If there's a glimpse of hope, the temptation is to take the bull by the horns and do everything in your power to salvage what's left.

You strive with all your might to make any kind of progress or advancement in the area you are most desperate in.

However, your strength and abilities only take you so far. When you're feeling brave or are desperate enough, you'll ask for help to fill a need, which is wise. You weren't meant to do life on your own. Others can often help take you places you couldn't get to on your own, but even then, they have limits too. If you're fortunate, a friend will say, "I'll do anything for you. You always have access to me, and I'll give you anything you need—a listening ear, money. Ask and it's yours." And on the rare occasion when you do hear this from someone, you wonder if they are able to come through and help to the full extent that you need. Other times, people give you the minimum, or you yourself give the minimum. It's easy for a person to have the attitude of "I'm busy, tired, and have limited resources. How little can I get by with giving you?"

But even with someone's help, there are aches and longings that people will never see or feel that are so alive in you. It can feel overwhelming when these are not fulfilled or satisfied, which can then lead to discontentment, discouragement, doubt, and hopelessness.

> *He hears your prayers and is working on your behalf.*

The good news is that just because the world can't see your aching heart, longings, and desires, it doesn't mean they're unseen. God sees. He doesn't stop at just "seeing"; He hears your prayers and is working on your behalf. This can be hard to believe, especially when you don't see your situation changing. Rest assured, He's not a distant God or father. He doesn't say, "Good luck with that," or

"Work really hard to achieve that yourself." Our heavenly Father enjoys giving us gifts, and they don't come with a price tag or strings attached.

> Every good and perfect gift is from above,
> coming down from the Father of the heavenly
> lights, who does not change like shifting
> shadows.
> – James 1:17

> "Which of you, if your son asks for bread, will give
> him a stone? Or if he asks for a fish, will give him
> a snake? If you, then, though you are evil, know
> how to give good gifts to your children, how much
> more will your Father in heaven give good gifts to
> those who ask him!"
> – Matthew 7:9–11

Have you ever received a gift at Christmas you were underwhelmed by? That you secretly wanted to return to the store but didn't have the heart to tell the gift giver? Have you had a gift that came in the mail broken from shipment mishandling? Have you had a birthday, wedding, shower, or another event you were going to and felt obligated to buy and bring a gift? Or maybe you were excited to buy a gift, but it felt burdensome because it cost money you didn't have?

Perfect gifts from a perfect motive come from above. God's finances don't change like yours. God's resources don't change like yours. He has the

Perfect gifts from a perfect motive come from above.

time to craft something specific to you and not a replica that hundreds of other people have received. His gifts to you are as unique as you are.

But there are times you have an expectation of what His good gifts or miracles should look like. I believe you have experienced many more miracles than you're aware of because you thought it would come in a different package, at a different time, or be more "thrilling."

The Bible talks about how God provided many miracles for the Israelites, a well-known one being the parting of the Red Sea. The Israelites were fleeing from Egypt, no longer wanting to be under Pharaoh's control. As they were running away, they came up against the Red Sea, and God miraculously spread the waters and they were able to walk through on dry land. As the Egyptians followed, the waters closed up on them. The Israelites sang songs of thanksgiving for how they were rescued. That would be considered a "big" miracle.

From there, the Israelites were on their way to the land God promised them but first had to go through the wilderness to get there. Many times the Israelites complained because of the lack of food and water, even to the point of wishing they were back in Egypt where they were enslaved and treated cruelly! So, God heard the cries of the Israelites and provided manna (bread), a food they had never seen before. They were dissatisfied. It tasted plain, looked plain, and not what they had in mind. And yet, it was a gift from heaven. It was a miracle. Without God's doing, it wouldn't have appeared, and they would have nothing to eat and sustain them.

The Israelites needed both the parting of the Red Sea

and the manna to remain alive and continue the journey. However, we usually only like to talk about the Red Sea miracle and forget about the manna miracle because it's less flashy. At face value it didn't seem to be anything special. Their lack of gratitude upset the Lord because He was providing them with a good gift, but they didn't recognize it as that. It wasn't enough, they wanted more, and yet it was exactly what they needed to continue their journey forward.

So as you pray to God for a gift or miracle in your life, remember to thank Him for not only the Red Sea miracles but also for the manna miracles. You've likely even had a manna miracle today.

What Red Sea or manna miracles have you given up hope for?

What do you doubt He is able to do?

What do you desire but are scared to ask for?

> Then Jesus said to his disciples, "Truly I tell you, it is hard for someone who is rich to enter the kingdom of heaven. Again I tell you, it is easier for a camel to go through the eye of a needle than for someone who is rich to enter the kingdom of God."
>
> When the disciples heard this, they were greatly astonished and asked, "Who then can be saved?"
>
> Jesus looked at them and said, "With man this is impossible, but with God all things are possible."
>
> – Matthew 19:23–26

Jesus stated a fact that some things are simply impossible for man to achieve, even for someone who is rich and has numerous resources and connections. And then there comes the "but." He doesn't leave you in an impossible state. He says, "But with God all things are possible"—"all" as in *everything*.

Can we just define *impossible* for a moment? Impossible: out of the question, unfeasible, unworkable, irrational, impractical, inconceivable, farfetched, unachievable.

- God can do the out of the question.
- God can do the unfeasible.
- God can do the unworkable.
- God can do the irrational.
- God can do the impractical.
- God can do the inconceivable.
- God can do the farfetched.
- God can do the unachievable.
- God can do the *impossible*.

Take a moment to think of things you desire that you've placed in the impossible category—those things you've thrown in a box, slapped a label with the word "impossible" on the side, and then stored in the attic because you've given up hope they will ever change or come to fruition. What things have you deemed no longer worth your time, energy, or tears?

> *God has done impossible things in the past, so who says He can't do them again?*

"*But* with God"—thank goodness for that statement. It tells you it's not the end. God has done impossible things in the past, so who says He can't do them again? Who says your situation is out of God's reach? God is not strapped or bound in any way; He is unlimited and uninhibited. This is hard to imagine because you and I are strapped for time, energy, and resources. We only have so much fuel in our tanks, so much so that we were designed to sleep, lay flat, and be "unproductive" for several hours every day.

Thank goodness He doesn't sleep. He is always available when we need Him.

> He will not let your foot slip—
> he who watches over you will not slumber;
> indeed, He who watches over Israel [and you]
> will neither slumber nor sleep.
> – Psalm 121:3–4

And He never stops working on your behalf.

> But Jesus replied, "My Father is always
> working, and so am I."
> – John 5:17 (NLT)

In fact, there's never any need to be frantic because He is not only your provider but your advocate. He advocates for your physical, emotional, mental, and spiritual needs and health, for restored relationships, for peace. Your good and perfect heavenly Father is faithful in these things regardless of if you followed all the rules that week, made good business decisions, or completed every item on your checklist.

Will you trust and believe that He has not forgotten about you and your needs?

Will you trust that He is able?

Will you trust that He is for you?

Will you believe that He can make the impossible, possible?

God's Heart to You

My child, I know your needs. I know you well and have been with you since the beginning, providing good gifts. I've been working, I am working and will continue to work in your life because you are My workmanship. You are My beloved. I'm not stingy with My resources, like you may have experienced from those around you. I don't tease or play games. I'm your Father and your provider. Don't fret or worry about tomorrow.

Know that My heart for you is good. Those things you are waiting on and yearning and fighting for, trust Me with them. I have a sweet and thought-out plan for your life, and I am working all things together for your good. You cannot fully fathom what I have in store for you.

I am your potter—let Me continue to shape those dreams.

Throw away your worry.

Loosen your grip.

Rest.

Relax.

Trust.

Believe Me.

I'm holding you.

I'm holding the impossible.

Think of your current circumstances from My perspective, not from the world's viewpoint or from your own ability. Think and trust Me beyond those borders of doubt you've created. Absolutely nothing is impossible for Me. Nothing.

So pray to Me big prayers—I can handle it. There are times you asked for too little because you weren't sure I could deliver. You asked for something that looked possible in your eyes. Again, I say, ask mighty and impossible things of Me. That's My specialty. That's where My glory shines.

It's My joy as a Father to give.

Can I knock your socks off?

Can I knock your socks off?

☐ NO, I'M NOT CONFIDENT YOU ARE ABLE TO DO
THE IMPOSSIBLE IN MY LIFE. I THINK I CAN FIND
A WAY TO MAKE THESE THINGS HAPPEN ON MY
OWN.

GOD: What things appear to be impossible in your
life right now? What doubts do you have about My ability to come through for you? I know it is tempting to
take matters into your own hands, but know that I am
capable of anything and I want to bless you.

☐ YES, I AM READY TO HAVE MY SOCKS KNOCKED
OFF! THANK YOU IN ADVANCE FOR WHAT YOU
ARE ABOUT TO DO!

GOD: Wonderful! Continue to trust and obey Me,
and I will lead you through wonders. Amid these wonders, I don't want you to forget how I see you and made
you in my image.

13

Can I Tell You How Great You Are?

Think of yourself approaching the end of a long day. You've done what you do most days—ran errands, worked at your job, attended to family, friends, and co-workers, completed some chores—and are now about to climb into bed. You lie down, and even though your body is still, your mind hasn't stopped running. You take in a deep breath, feel a sense of relief, and think, *Wow, I really accomplished a lot today. I feel good about myself. Way to go, self— you were a success!* Or maybe your breathing is ragged, and you're feeling defeated and thinking, *Wow, I really messed up. I didn't get x, y and z done, so-and-so is upset with me, and I underperformed. I'm no good.*

Then you wake up the next morning, place your feet on the floor, and start moving again. You may have a bounce in your step, an upright posture, and be thinking, *I don't know what today is going to bring, but I know I can handle it. God will help me get through the challenges that lie ahead of me to-*

day. I can do this! Or you may have your head hung low, and you're dragging your feet and thinking, *I don't know if I have what it takes. I'm not enough. What if I mess up and disappoint myself and others again today? I'm not sure I can do this. Does the world really need me?*

There's a story you tell yourself every day about who you are and what your worth is. Your worth is constantly being measured and compared. How you see yourself can change hour by hour, minute by minute.

If you were to write an entire book describing to the world who you are, what would you say? How would you describe your personality, physical attributes, character, accomplishments, passions, failures, gifts, and so on? Think on this for a couple of minutes. After reading your own book. . .

Are you inspired?

Are you proud of yourself?

Do you like or dislike yourself?

Does your book carry a tone of honor and celebration or defeat and pessimism?

Now, what if your family, friends, and co-workers were to write a book describing who you are? How would the book you wrote compare to theirs? I'm guessing some things would be similar, and some things would surprise you because you would never have said or thought those things about yourself. What is true? What is factual? You might ask yourself, *What and who do I believe? Am I right, or do they see a part of me that I don't?*

I'm not sure what you've heard about yourself over the course of your life from parents, siblings, teachers, friends, co-workers, strangers, and social media, but these varied and ever-changing voices have been speaking to you since the day you were born. Over time, these thoughts and opinions have been so ingrained in you that you have allowed them to shape you and your identity. You end up living according to those opinions. You have the tendency to let them have a say in who you are and what your worth is.

Your circumstances can also influence how you see yourself. Have the following life circumstances and labels affected how you view or feel about yourself, for better or worse?

- Single. Married. Divorced. Separated.
- Many friendships. A couple of friendships. No friendships.
- Good paying job. Struggling to keep job. Laid off or fired.
- Big house. Little house. Renting. Living with parents. Homeless.
- A lot of money in savings account. Little or no money in savings account.
- Specific life goals. Feel lost, unsure of next steps.
- Very efficient. Not productive enough.
- Educated. Uneducated. Straight A student. Hoping to graduate.
- A clean criminal record. Fines, convictions, felonies.
- Healthy. Battling a chronic disease or addiction.
- Optimal weight. Overweight.
- Good hair day. Bad hair day.

You've likely experienced some of the good and bad in many of the above circumstances. These circumstances can change back and forth many times in a day, week, or year. Does how you see yourself change and shift as often as these circumstances? One moment you love yourself because you think you are doing well in life. You have a job you are succeeding at, you haven't had any recent fights with family and friends, you exercised a couple of times this week, and you checked off most things on the to-do list. You think, *Today was productive. I'm feeling pretty good about myself!* On another day, your boss scolds you, there's a family dispute, your neighbor makes a complaint about not keeping up your yard, you lose your cool with a customer service representative, you don't reply to your friend who reached out four days ago, and you're having a bad hair day and simply feeling insecure. You think, *I underperformed. I can't keep up. I don't like who I am.*

There are many voices speaking to you. Your own voice and what others say about you. The voices of those you know and don't know. The voices of your circumstances. And they all speak very loud! As you continually hear these voices, whose voices are you truly listening to? Whose voices are you allowing to speak into your life and influence what you believe? Thank goodness there's another voice that is pure and honest. God's voice—the one that says who you really are. His voice is most accurate because He is the one who created every part of you and knows you intimately. No part of you is hidden from Him.

> You formed my innermost being, shaping my
> delicate inside and my intricate outside, and
> wove them all together in my mother's womb.
> I thank you, God, for making me so
> mysteriously complex!
> Everything you do is marvelously
> breathtaking.

It simply amazes me to think about it!
How thoroughly you know me, Lord!
You even formed every bone in my body
when you created me in the secret place,
carefully, skillfully shaping me from nothing
to something.
You saw who you created me to be before I
became me!
Before I'd ever seen the light of day,
the number of days you planned for me
were already recorded in your book.
Every single moment you are thinking of me!
How precious and wonderful to consider
that you cherish me constantly in your every
thought!
O God, your desires toward me are more
than the grains of sand on every shore!
When I awake each morning, you're still with
me.
– Psalm 139:13–18 (TPT)

God made you and me unique. In a world where there's
constant comparison and competition, you often don't see
yourself as special. You think you would be more likable and
accepted if you were more like that other person everyone
sees as important or amazing. However, no one has the same
DNA, fingerprints, or heartbeat as you do. And despite the
many personality tests out there, you are much more than a
"personality type." He has given you spiritual gifts, passions,
purposes, and desires that are unique to you.

There has never been or will ever be another *you*!

> *There has never been or will ever be another you!*

When it comes to your identity and who you are, you gravitate toward associating with certain things or people to form your identity. There's a natural pull to attach or belong to something of importance. The options of where you can place your identity are limitless! You can put your identity or worth in your job, socioeconomic status, education level, the company you work for, the area of town you live in, your material possessions, physical attributes, relationship status, awards, hobbies, friend groups, your last name, and so on. All these things are part of your life, but they are not who you are because, as you know, some of these things can change as easily as the weather.

Your identity was never meant to fluctuate based on your circumstances or how good or bad life is going. When you surrender your life to God and choose to live for Him, you become His son or daughter. Your identity is no longer in your job. It is now *in Christ Jesus*. Your job no longer has the authority to tell you how important you are. Your material possessions or life savings do not get to tell you what your life is worth. Your standing with Jesus doesn't change based your current mood or accomplishments. Your standing with Him stays the same. Jesus now has the say in who you are.

Your identity in and through Jesus means that:

- You are fiercely loved without condition.
- Shame and condemnation have no hold on you.
- You are no longer a slave or controlled by sin; you are free!
- You are a new creation. He sees you as clean and

pure.

- The Holy Spirit lives in you, giving you His wisdom, power, fruit, and gifts.
- You are more than a conqueror through Jesus's power.
- You are made right with God.
- You are an heir of God.
- You are no longer an orphan; you are a child of God.

You are not great because your mom says you are great. You are great because you are His. He made you, He thinks of you, loves you, and redeems you. He will never disown you as His child. His favor rests on you.

> *He made you, He thinks of you, loves you, and redeems you.*

But to all who believed him and accepted him,
he gave the right to become children of God.
 – John 1:12 (NLT)

As you begin to listen to and believe who God says you are, all other voices and opinions start to grow strangely dim. There will be no need to strive for approval anymore—you are stamped with His love and favor.

God's Heart to You

Since you were born, you've had a multitude of voices speaking into your life about who you are and who you're not. You have rehearsed these words and opinions over and over in your mind. Many have taken root. They've started to reframe how you live and how you view yourself. This has left you feeling confined under a label that has been placed on you.

You have been labeled unworthy, not enough, and weak, and branded a failure.

When you invite My presence and My voice to speak to who you are, these labels no longer have the power to stick to you. They do not get to tell you who you are. I do. My favor and opinion of you does not change like you have experienced with the world.

As My child, not only do you have My love but you have My power. Your weakness does not diminish My power—in fact, that's where it's greatest. My power is perfected in this very place. You don't have to achieve anything on your own. You don't have to measure up or prove your worth to Me. I've already made your worth immeasurable.

Some have overlooked you, but I never have. You are the apple of My eye.

I am for you. I am fighting for you. You are secure with Me. I don't need to see your resume. Regardless of your earthly success or failure, I love you the same. The exact same.

Let Me open your eyes to every label and belief that is not from Me. I'll not only remove and destroy them but replace them until your images and My images are alike.

With Me, there is freedom from your old self.

With Me, you will discover who you really are and how I designed you.

Can I tell you how great you are?

Can I tell you how great you are?

☐ No, I THINK I ALREADY KNOW WHO I AM AND DON'T WANT ANY MORE VOICES CONFUSING MY IDENTITY.

GOD: I have known you before you were born. I know you inside and out. You are so precious to Me. I will never lie to you or discourage you. I bring clarity into your identity. When you are ready, I am here to speak life into your life.

☐ YES, I WANT TO HEAR MORE ABOUT HOW YOU SEE ME AND CAN HELP ME UNDERSTAND MY WORTH.

GOD: There's so much more I want you to discover about how I made you. There is so much beauty and potential inside you, and I can't wait for your eyes to be opened to it. Now that you are beginning to see yourself through My eyes, I also want to tell you more about who I am as well.

14

Can I Tell You How Great I Am?

Have you ever talked with someone, and throughout the conversation, it seemed as though they were reading off their resume? They mentioned their job titles, leadership positions, awards, and the big things they will tackle soon. Without perhaps even knowing it, they wanted you to know these things so you'd think highly of them and they'd gain your approval. This information wasn't necessarily for your benefit but more for theirs. You leave the conversation feeling unnoticed and unknown. And the slight aroma of a prideful spirit follows them.

Who doesn't want to be noticed and seen as important? You feel that the hours, blood, sweat, and tears should be recognized. That title you worked so hard for shouldn't be all for nothing, right?

Being known, seen, celebrated, and applauded are not bad things. Many times, they are very well deserved. But a selfish heart starts to form when a person's sole motivation is to seek these accolades to elevate themselves while neglecting to call out the greatness in others.

When God describes His greatness, He is simply stating who He is. Many things and people are vying for your attention, adoration, and worship but when you get a true glimpse of His character and who He is, a natural praise follows. Whether intentional or unintentional, many do not truthfully portray Him, and He wants to set the record straight. He's not like other "gods." He doesn't need your reassurance and applause to feel good about Himself. Knowing Him is for your benefit. He wants to be your God. How do you call on someone you don't know or trust?

If you asked a hundred people on the street, "Who is God, and what is He like?" you would hear a whole array of responses. They would be even more varied if you asked this question to people from different states, countries, cultures, and religions. We would hear everything from "He doesn't exist" to "He is the one true God" and a million answers and descriptions in between.

If someone walked up to you on the street and asked, "Who is God, and what is He like?" how would you personally respond? And think not only of how would you respond in terms of your verbal spiel, but what type of response happened inside you when that question was asked? Did you get nervous or uncomfortable, have your guard up, and were unsure of how to answer? Were you annoyed that the person would ask such a personal question? Did you light up and get excited to engage in this topic? Did you feel confident about who you believe God to be and comfortable about what He is like?

There's both an internal and external response to this

question. Does your internal response match your outer response? Are you angry and distant with God internally but speak rosy words on the outside? Or do you love God internally but don't feel like you could express that outwardly? Take a moment to take inventory of how your heart and mind respond to that question.

Regardless of someone's background or where they are from, when one tries to describe God, the response is often influenced from the things they have heard from others and their life experiences.

Over the years, what have your parents, teachers, friends, pastor or spiritual leader, colleagues, or social media influencers said about who God is? They may have talked your ear off about God or maybe never mentioned Him. You may have heard about Him in a positive or negative tone. If you trusted and respected that person, you likely took what they said to heart and didn't doubt it much. If you didn't respect or have a good relationship with this person, you probably questioned their opinion and it fell flat.

And what about those life experiences? Life can simply be unfair and unkind, to say the least. Most of us have experienced a death in the family, a strained relationship, a loss that left our heart broken, a chronic health condition, mental health struggles, and being overlooked and mistreated. During these times, we aim many questions at God such as:

- Are You going to help me through this?
- Why did You let this happen?
- Have You forsaken me or forgotten about me?
- Are You still good, or were You ever good?
- Can I trust You?

These painful experiences and questions can lead you

down a couple different paths. One path you may have traveled down is to further doubt who He is, to be so discouraged that the best way you know to remove yourself from this confusion is to turn around and walk the other direction and to stiff-arm God and subconsciously choose to trust what makes sense in your head. Another path you may have traveled down is to sit in the tension, to wrestle with all the things that logically don't make sense, to be truly honest with how you're feeling and your doubts and fears, and to continue to ask more questions.

Choosing what path or direction to go with your doubts and questions is like diving into the ocean. As you look down, it's unclear, unknown, and scary. But as you go further down, you see things you have never seen before, a whole new world that always existed but you are now just finding. The deeper you go, the more you find. Or you can conclude that it's too scary and too unknown and not worth the risk, while making the choice to return to the surface where you're surrounded by what's familiar, predictable, and safe. No fear, no fog.

In your spiritual ocean dive, where are you going? Are you diving deeper, or are you swimming to the surface, about to get out of the water?

Dear friend (I feel like I can call you that since we've been on this journey for a while now), I see you in the ocean, anxiously fluttering your arms and legs, wanting to get out of the tension of all the questions, pain, confusion, and conflicting messages. Relax. I encourage you to make a bold move and turn your gaze not to the surface but to the deep. You don't need to make any sudden moves or make big decisions, just turn your gaze. I know the surface looks so appealing right now. You just want to get out of the middle, out of the muck. But the surface has nothing new for you. In the deep, there's exploration. There's beauty. There's adventure. In the deep, there are more questions and more answers.

God is calling you to go deeper with Him. He knows it is uncomfortable for you, but He is asking because He has more to show you about Himself and more to show you about who you are, how He created you, and His plans for you. If you stop now, so does the growth.

> *God is calling you to go deeper with Him.*

You have multitudes of thoughts and opinions about God that birthed out of what others have told you and your life experiences. But who better to tell about who God is than God Himself? If the world were learning about you, you would want the facts and narrative to come from you. God is the same. Let Him tell you who He is.

Just as you have a name and possibly a handful of nicknames, God also has a name. But He doesn't have just one name; He has many. And each name of His reveals another dimension of who He is.

Even though Jesus knew who He was, He asked His disciples what they thought of Him. Jesus was not looking for confirmation, a boost of self-confidence, or reassurance of who He was. He wanted to know what was in the heart of His disciples. He wanted to connect with them on a deeper level.

> He asked his disciples, "Who do people say the Son of Man is?"

They replied, "Some say John the Baptist; others say Elijah; and still others, Jeremiah or one of the prophets."

"But what about you?" he asked. "Who do you say I am?"

Simon Peter answered, "You are the Messiah, the Son of the living God."

Jesus replied, "Blessed are you, Simon son of Jonah, for this was not revealed to you by flesh and blood, but by my Father in heaven."

– Matthew 16:13–17

As you just read, people had a variety of answers to the question "Who do you say the Son of Man is?" In a world of gray, here there was one right answer: "You are the Messiah, the Son of the living God."

Throughout the Bible, God is not only labeled many different names but He *is* those names. God is more than a noun; He is a verb. As you read some of His names below, don't just see them as titles, but see Him acting these names out in your life. He is "being" these things for you. He is the *living* God.

> *God is more than a noun; He is a verb.*

God Most High (El Elyon)

Creator, Mighty and Strong (Elohim)

Everlasting God (El Olam)

The Lord. I AM. (Yahweh)

Daddy, Father (Abba)

The LORD Our Shepherd (Yahweh Rohi)

The LORD Will Provide (Yahweh Yireh)

The LORD Is Peace (Yahweh Shalom)
The God Who Heals (Jehovah Rapha)
The LORD Is My Banner (Yahweh Nissi)
The God Who Sees Me (El Roi)
Jealous (Qanna)

And here are even more of God's character traits and attributes:

- Infinite – He is the beginning and the end.
- Immutable – He never changes.
- Self-sufficient – He has no needs.
- Omnipotent – He is all-powerful.
- Omniscient – He is all-knowing.
- Omnipresent – He is always everywhere.
- Wise – He is full of perfect, unchanging wisdom.
- Faithful – He is unchanging and always comes through.
- Good – He is kind.
- Just – He is right and perfect in all He does.
- Merciful – He is compassionate and kind, doesn't give us what we deserve.
- Gracious – He gives us what we don't deserve.
- Loving – He is love, and His love is unconditional.
- Holy – He is perfect and set apart.
- Glorious – He is beautiful and great.
- Miracle worker – He does the impossible.
- Promise keeper – He stays true to His word.
- Does not get weary, doesn't sleep – He always works on your behalf.
- Never leaves or forsakes – He is ever-present and faithful.
- Protects and defends – He fights on our behalf.
- Redeems – He takes what is broken and makes it new.

- Forgiver – He removes the debt of our sin.
- Emmanuel – God is present with us.
- Giver – He blesses us with good things.

God is not only all these things but He embodies all of these traits continuously and perfectly. This is hard to imagine because you and I are not perfect and we haven't experienced anything or anyone who is. Each one of us has faltered, sinned, and has had moments of not following through on our promises. But He has not. There are times when it appears as though He has forgotten about you or does not appear to be good. God's great enemy, Satan, would love for you to believe that God is not true to His word or character.

Your feelings and circumstances and the voices in this world aim to grab on to your beliefs and yank them around. There was one time in particular where my circumstance was challenging my belief in God. One minute I believed in the character and goodness of God, and the next minute I didn't. Peace came, followed by anxiety, and back and forth it went. I felt like God gently stopped me in my tracks and clearly asked me, "Am I your God or not?" He didn't ask in a condemning way but was sincerely asking where I stood with Him. Either I trust Him, or I don't. Either I believe He is my provider, or I don't. Either I believe He is faithful, or I don't. Either I believe He is for me, or I don't. And on it goes.

Either I believe He is actively "being" these things in this current moment, or I don't. Can you imagine if a close friend one minute tells you they trust you, and the next minute doubts your word, character, and loyalty? What if your friend changes their mind about you as often as the wind changes directions? This would be a very unstable and unhealthy relationship.

God knows you struggle with doubt and that you can easily go astray. This is why the Bible mentions many times for you to "renew" your mind.

> Do not conform to the pattern of this world,
> but be transformed by the renewing of
> your mind. Then you will be able to test
> and approve what God's will is—his good,
> pleasing and perfect will.
> – Romans 12:2

> Set your minds on things above, not on
> earthly things.
> – Colossians 3:2

Your relationship with God is one of grace, which means you don't have to earn your way to Him. You don't have to be good enough for Him. Your deeds do not land on a scale of good and bad, where if you perform more good than bad deeds you go to heaven and vice versa. He accepts you as you are with all the good, bad, and ugly combined. When you choose to surrender yourself to Him and follow Him, you get all of Him. All the traits and names of God you read above are all for you.

The Bible says there is no one like Him. The gods of other religions cannot even be put in the same category as Him.

> *When you choose to surrender yourself to Him and follow Him, you get all of Him.*

> For the LORD your God is God of gods and
> Lord of lords, the great God, mighty and
> awesome.
> – Deuteronomy 10:17

He created the universe. He can raise the dead. He is the beginning and the end.

His greatness is beyond our human comprehension.

He doesn't call you to understand Him; He calls you to trust Him.

He calls you to walk by faith and follow Him on this journey He has you on.

He calls you to rest in the fact the He acts and moves on your behalf.

He calls you to believe He is who He says He is—because He is.

God's Heart to You

Over the years, you've heard many things about Me from the world around you. Some have said I'm just another god, one of many that can be worshiped and followed. Some have said that My Son, Jesus, was just a good man and teacher. And some sidestep my Holy Spirit because He is just a little too unfamiliar for them. Along the way, your life experiences have challenged your view of My character.

So, with all this, who do *you* say that I am?

These views and opinions of Me have put layer upon layer of scales on your eyes. It has begun to callous your heart, and doubt is never far off. This has created apathy and distance from Me.

Renewing is one of My specialties. I love taking what is old and making it new again. I love taking what was wrong and making it right again. I love not only restoring but upgrading.

Will you let Me do this renewing work with your eyes to help you see Me more clearly?

Will you let Me do this renewing work with your mind to help you know what is true about Me?

Will you let Me do this renewing work with your heart and emotions to help you let Me in and accept my peace?

I want you to see that I am like no other. I am the one true God, above every other god. My name is above every other name. Nothing is too hard for Me; nothing is impossible for Me. I hold victory in My hands. I fight for My children. I am a shelter and a refuge when trouble chases you. I am the perfect and wise Counselor. I am fully trustworthy. I make all things new. I make a way when there is no way. I am hope. I am abundant life, and I offer it to you. I am love, and I love you.

Can I tell you how great I am?

Can I tell you how great I am?

☐ NO, I AM STILL DOUBTING AND WRESTLING
   WITH WHO YOU ARE.

GOD: I reassure you, if you wait until you have no doubts about Me before you draw closer, you will never come. Come with your doubts and questions. Tell Me more about what they are as well as your experiences that have influenced how you view Me.

☐ YES, PLEASE TELL ME MORE ABOUT YOUR
   GREATNESS. I WANT TO KNOW YOU MORE!

GOD: Even though the extent of My ways and My greatness cannot fully be fathomed, I will continue to open your eyes and heart to all that I am along this journey we are on. The ultimate invitation is coming, the invitation for Me to be your one and only.

15

Can I Be Your One and Only?

Options, choices, decisions, oh my! Every day you must make dozens of decisions with many options, from small, minor choices like what to eat and what to wear to major, weighty decisions such as what job to take, where to live, and who to marry.

There are choices you make by default, like the roads you take to work or the shampoo you buy. These are not difficult decisions to make and are typically the same week to week. Other times you analyze all options, write out a "pros vs. cons" list, gather several opinions, and do your research before you choose which option is best. Decision-making can bring anxiety based on fear of choosing incorrectly or going down a wrong path. You may find yourself stuck in indecision and fearing you'll miss out on what is best for you.

Even though it can be difficult to decide between many different options, it is healthy to do so. Can you imagine if you bought ten different bottles of shampoo and used a different one each day because you couldn't commit to one brand? Or you became homeless because you couldn't decide what apartment, house, or city to live in, so you chose none of them? These examples may sound silly, but to some degree, most of us struggle with indecision and finally *choosing* an option.

Many people think there's freedom in keeping options open and not committing to one thing. But in doing so, you forfeit everything that comes with commitment and going fully in with that one thing or person. You lose expertise, depth, substance, history, and being known when you choose to dabble versus delving in.

Are you treating your faith the same way? You might be thinking, *How can I choose just one option? What if I pick the wrong faith, religion, or god? Can I just dabble a little in each religion and piece together what makes sense to me and my way of life? And so, careful not offend anyone, I will say they are all good, all okay, and all acceptable.*

But what if these different faiths and religions that claim to be true actually contradict each other? It would make it challenging to follow several religions or gods if one is saying, "This is the way. Follow me!" and the other is saying, "No, this is the way. Follow me!" If five different people say they are president of the United States, you know that four of them are either lying or are cons because there can only be one president. Or imagine you had several supervisors at your job and they were all giving you different directions and different orders and had different expectations? It would be exceedingly difficult to do your job well when you must follow several leaders. There's more productivity, clarity, efficiency, and advancement when you follow one leader and listen to one voice.

Most religions lead you down a particular path and require you to follow their leader or god. In a sense, they all say, "Choose me; choose this way." The God of the Bible doesn't give a multiple-choice answer of "all of the above" when it comes to choosing which god or religion to follow. He says He is the God of gods and the Lord of lords. He says, "There is no other besides Me." He says His Son, Jesus, is the way and the truth and the life. God says Jesus is the gateway, where life, freedom, and salvation can be found.

> *God says Jesus is the gateway, where life, freedom, and salvation can be found.*

All this may sound limiting, restrictive, and demanding to some. But God says that choosing to follow only Him, and choosing this one option, actually leads to more freedom, not less. He gives you freedom from trying to be good enough and earning your way to Him; freedom from the shame of your sin, letting Jesus, not you, do the redeeming and cleansing; freedom from your past; freedom from striving to make things happen in your own strength; freedom from rules, rituals, and traditions.

There's no finger-pointing with God, only a welcoming embrace. He wants to be your Father, and you His child. You will not be a slave to Him but a friend.

> *There's no finger-pointing with God, only a welcoming embrace.*

For those who are led by the Spirit of God are the children of God. The Spirit you received

does not make you slaves, so that you live
in fear again; rather, the Spirit you received
brought about your adoption to sonship.
And by him we cry, "*Abba*, Father." The
Spirit himself testifies with our spirit that we
are God's children. Now if we are children,
then we are heirs—heirs of God and co-
heirs with Christ, if indeed we share in his
sufferings in order that we may also share in
his glory.

— Romans 8:14–17

There are many parties you may never get invited to and
many icons you will never meet. But there's an invitation
that has already been sent to you. It has your name on it. It is
lying open before you, waiting for your RSVP. If you decide
to go, you will get to meet, know, and experience the best of
the best: God, Jesus, and the Holy Spirit.

You get to partner with them for life. Running your
race with them will look new and different as you move forward. You will no longer be lost and running aimlessly but
will run with intention, focus, and purpose. You will have a
calling that He will give you to live out. You will no longer
be striving to please everyone, and your eyes will be fixed
ahead and not in the past—fixed on eternal things that last
and not temporal, earthly, and frivolous things. You will no
longer be dragging your sin along with you. No more shackles on your feet. Your renewed heart and mind will see the
world around you from His perspective. Loving and serving
will be your anthem. You will have an audience of One. His
words and His counsel will guide you and remind you who

you are. His voice is full of truth and is life-giving. And with Him, even joy and hope can be had in the darkest of trials.

This is life with Him.

This day, who will you choose to follow?

Who will you trust with your surrender?

God's Heart to You

I am jealous for you. Each time you look to another person or thing to validate who you are, I burn with holy jealousy. When you listen to another's voice to speak into your identity, you begin to conform, and the uniqueness, creativity and calling I've instilled in you becomes hard to recognize. This saddens Me because I have great plans for you and a future full of hope for you. But when you listen to My voice it will breathe new life in you and allow you to fulfill the purpose I have for you.

There's so much that I am and want to be for you.

I can be anywhere, and I want to be near you and you near to Me.

I am a great listener, and I want to listen to you.

I am the voice of truth, and I want to speak to you.

I am perfect love, and I want to love you to pieces.

I am where freedom is, and I want to set you free.

I am all-powerful and full of wisdom, and I want to put that same power and wisdom in you.

I am clothed in righteousness, and I want to clothe you in the same way.

I am a leader, and I want to shepherd you.

I am a defender, and I want to fight for you.

I bring life, and I want to carry your burdens and remove your anxiety and fear.

I am patient, and I want to walk with you in the waiting.

I am a miracle worker, and I want to make a way for you where there is no way.

I am Creator, and I want to remind you who you are and how I created you.

I am the God of gods and the Lord of lords, and I want to be everything I am to you.

I am your heavenly Father, and I want to be yours and I want you to be mine.

I am God, and I am your Abba Father. Will you loosen your grip and let Me be these things for you? I know your heart is prone to wander and turn elsewhere. And at times, it does. The further you wander, the deeper your heart aches. And it's telling you, you are homesick.

Your heart's home is with Me.

Can I be your God?

Can I be your one and only?

Can I be your one and only?

☐ NO, I AM NOT READY TO CHOOSE ONLY ONE GOD TO SERVE AND COMMIT TO.

GOD: This breaks My heart, but I will wait for you and keep pursuing you. I have chosen you for great purposes. I am here to meet you with open arms when you decide to choose Me in return.

☐ YES, GOD, I CHOOSE YOU. YOU ARE MY ONE AND ONLY. I WILL LOVE AND SERVE YOU FOR THE REST OF MY DAYS. THANK YOU FOR LOVING ME UNCONDITIONALLY. THANK YOU FOR BEING MY GOD.

GOD: This delights Me more than you know. I, as well as legions of angels, am rejoicing at this very moment. I will be your God till the very end. Welcome home.

Application Guide

For individual reflection, mentorship support,
or group discussion use.

Throughout this book, God asks, "Can I be your God?" regarding all areas of your life, for the rest of your life. But what would it look like to invite God into a specific area of your life? To walk through a challenging situation, struggle, or hardship with Him instead of navigating it on your own? This is where the rubber meets the road.

The following section will help you apply even more deeply and specifically the ways God is inviting you to connect with Him. I challenge you to dive into the fifteen questions God asked you throughout this book and use them to help process the things you're navigating in your life.

You can process these questions in many ways, but I especially encourage you to process "out loud." Instead of keeping everything inside you, untangle those thoughts and feelings by writing them out on paper (blank pages are provided in this section), talking through them with a close friend or mentor, or discussing them in a group setting with people who may be going through similar life circumstances. Ultimately, it's about developing a relationship with your heavenly Father, who deeply cares for you. Let Him show you how He wants to be your God, and embrace the journey with Him.

Things to consider as you use this guide:

Name your struggle or trial. What is on your mind constantly that you can't seem to fix, make headway in, or are confused about? What part of your life feels heavy, defeating, and heartbreaking? That "thing" may be acute but seasonal (days or weeks), such as a difficult work situation, an argument with a friend, or fear of starting something new, or it may be chronic and long lasting (months or years), such as anxiety and depression, an ongoing addiction, a struggling marriage, or a prolonged waiting period.

Pray. Prayer is communication with God, both speaking and listening to Him. Don't rely on logic or how the world around you says to "fix" your life. You are here for divine insight, wisdom, and counsel from the Holy Spirit. Communicate with Him throughout your processing (before, during, and after).

Applying the questions. This is a time to process with God a difficult situation, circumstance, or trial in your life. Be honest with God in your answers and conversation with Him. Your response may not be clean, concise, or pretty, and that's okay. If more questions or doubts arise, express those to Him, and let it turn into a dialogue between the two of you.

No time limits. God could speak or reveal something to you in a second, or He may desire for you to go deeper with Him and experience hidden treasures that can only be found through "digging." You may cover one section per day, per week, or per month. Let God dictate the pace. Remember, the end goal is connection with Him.

No rules or boundaries. This guide is not a "homework" assignment. You do not need to answer every question in this guide. You might skip one question while another you meditate on for weeks. When writing or journaling, some people process through writing long paragraphs, and others work best through bullet points, key words that come to mind, or even drawing and doodling. Our relationship with God is unique, so each person may approach and use this guide slightly differently to connect with Him.

1. Can I meet with you?

- When was the last time you sought to connect with God? Or when did you feel like He was calling you to meet with Him?
- Is there anything that makes you hesitant or nervous to meet with Him about your life circumstances?
- How do you feel about God coming near to you, having full view of your heart and mind? Can you think of times you have pushed God away? If so, what were the circumstances surrounding those times, and why did you want to distance yourself from Him?
- Are you able, willing, and ready to go a little deeper with Him than you've done previously? If not, why not?
- What is the state of your soul (mind, will, and emotions) going into this meeting?
- What outcome are you hoping will result from meeting with him?

Remember, there's nowhere you can flee from His presence. He won't force you to meet with Him. All He wants is an open heart. He is ready and waiting to meet with you anywhere at any time.

> "Let us then with confidence draw near
> to the throne of grace, that we may receive
> mercy and find grace to help in time of
> need."
> —Heb. 4:16 ESV

2. Can I hear what you have to say?

- Have you talked with God yet about the things that
  concern you? If so, how often? And what forms of
  "talking" (internally or externally) do you do with
  Him (e.g., complaining, pleading, venting, asking
  why, requesting, praying, expressing gratitude, re-
  calling "truths," asking or giving forgiveness)? Continue to talk with Him.
- Express to God how you have felt during this time
  (e.g., are you anxious, depressed, fearful, frustrated,
  discouraged, angry, lost, despairing, offended, confused, hopeful, anticipatory, expectant, peaceful,
  contented, discontented, compassionate, relieved).
- Do you have specific questions you want to ask
  God but haven't yet? If so, what are they?

Remember, you are not talking to a wall; you are talking to the God of the universe who is alive and well and who has the capacity to hear and handle what you have to say. He cares. He is listening, leaning in, and focused in on what you are saying.

> "Morning, noon, and night I cry out in my
> distress, and the Lord hears my voice."
> —Psalm 55:17 NLT

3. Can I tell you something?

- When was the last time you stopped or slowed down to listen to what He has to say (from the Bible, Holy Spirit, promptings, convictions, etc.) about this situation?

- What is God's perspective on what you're going through? What does the Bible say about this specific trial or trials in general? Find and write out at least a couple of verses that bring you comfort and clarity during this time. Memorize and meditate on these verses.

- What have other voices in your life, including your own, been saying about your situation? What advice have they offered? Do those voices line up with what God is saying to you?

- What encouragement is God giving you? What direction or steps is He asking you to take or not take?

Remember, discerning between God's voice and Satan's voice is critical. Satan's voice includes words of shame, condemnation, and hopelessness. He rushes, pushes, frightens, intimidates, lies, and confuses you. God's voice is life giving, gracious, and convicting (making you aware of things you weren't aware of before). His voice calms, leads, and reassures you.

"Your word is a lamp for my feet, a light on my path."
—Psalm 119:105

4. Can I love you to pieces?

- Have you felt loved by God during this challenging time in your life? If so, how has He shown His love to you? If not, how have you not felt loved by Him?
- Do you ever feel like you don't measure up? If so, what areas of your life do you feel like you need to "be more of" to deserve God's and other people's love and acceptance?
- God so loved the world that He *gave* His one and only Son to die on the cross for you. Write what God has given you or wants to give you during this difficult time (e.g., encouragement, perseverance, insight, wisdom, strength, grace, forgiveness, hope, vision, a miracle). In what ways can you practically reflect His character by giving to others during this trial?

Remember, God is love, and even the greatest, most challenging situations you face cannot separate you from His fierce love for you. During these times (and always) He is patient, kind, not rude, not easily angered, keeps no records of wrongs, and loves you unconditionally.

> "This is how much God **loved** the world: **He gave** his Son, his one and only Son. And this is why: so that no one need be destroyed; by believing in him, anyone can have a whole and lasting life."
> —John 3:16 MSG

5. Can I make you free as a bird?

- Has this situation felt like having mud on your wings—are you feeling stuck, slow, hesitant, down-trodden? If so, identify the "mud." What is specifically weighing you down?
- How much extra weight is being put on you either from yourself or from those around you?
- Are you trying to attain perfection (in yourself or in others) during this challenging time? If so, in what ways?
- What areas of this situation are making you feel weak, tired, or hopeless? What encouragement is God speaking to you in these areas?
- Have you felt distant from God during this time? Do you know how or why this detachment came to be (e.g., sin, pain, questioning, doubting, unbelief, change of perspective)? Is there anything you would like to confess or express to God? Is there anything you need to let go of to gain the joy and freedom that Jesus wants you to experience?
- What personal transformation would you like to see in yourself on the other side of this trial?

Remember, it's His kindness that leads to repentance. You can approach His throne of grace with confidence, and He will redeem and make all things new!

"Therefore, if anyone is in Christ, the new creation has come: The old has gone, the new is here!"
—2 Corinthians 5:17

6. Can I make you powerful and wise?

- Can you recall moments you've operated out of your own knowledge, understanding, strength, and power in this trial? Are there times you've tried to control or manage parts of the chaos and dysfunction? If so, in what ways?
- In what ways do you need divine advice, counsel, wisdom, strength, and power from the Holy Spirit?
- What advice have others given you in hard times? How does it line up with the counsel of the Holy Spirit and what God says in His Word?
- What actions and emotions have come to the surface? Have you experienced anger, resentment, unforgiveness, shame, or anxiety? Love, joy, peace, patience, kindness, goodness, faithfulness, gentleness, or self-control?
- In what ways does God want to work miracles through you in this trial?

Remember, the Holy Spirit wants to counsel you as you walk through this journey. Take time to listen, and then act on what He is saying. You are not meant to do this on your own.

> "Now the Lord is the Spirit, and where the
> Spirit of the Lord is, there is freedom."
> —2 Corinthians 3:17

7. Can I give you a new wardrobe?

- What has been the condition of your soul (mind, will, and emotions) during recent hardships? Take time to break each one down:
  - ◊ Mind—What are your thoughts surrounding your circumstances? How are you thinking about yourself and about others who are involved? Have your thoughts been negative and despairing or hopeful and full of anticipation? Are you renewing your mind to believe what is true about this situation?
  - ◊ Will—What decisions (good or bad) have you made or are you planning to make? What has been the fruit of any decisions you've made?
  - ◊ Emotions—What emotions do these challenging times bring out in you? Have your emotions been acting as a gauge or a guide?
- What does it look like to "clothe yourself" in compassion, kindness, humility, gentleness, and patience? Which do you struggle with the most? If you are struggling with these qualities, don't force them. Check in with your thinking, and search for God's perspective.
- How are you integrating the gifts of the Holy Spirit into these times?

Remember, both your body and soul have a wardrobe. Your outward appearance and actions are a reflection of your heart and mind. Don't skip doing the inner work and healing with God, for this is the road to true beauty on all levels.

> "Therefore, as God's chosen people, holy and dearly loved, clothe yourselves with compassion, kindness, humility, gentleness and patience."
> —Colossians 3:12

8. Can I take you on an adventure?

- You may have a preferred destination in mind when it comes to seeing the end of your challenging situation. But how has the journey been? What are some of the ups and downs you've experienced? What roadblocks, detours, interruptions, unexpected surprises, and blessings have come out of the journey so far?

- How have you seen God daily provide for you through this adventurous journey?

- How has He shaped and refined you so far? What has He taught you along the way?

- Has anything caused you to stumble or slow down on your journey? If so, what is it, and are you willing to let go of it so you can run your race more freely?

- Has your perseverance, stamina, and resilience grown because of these hardships? If so, in what ways?

- Are you willing to stay in step with God into the unknown future? Do you trust Him with this adventure?

Remember, He has not stopped writing your story. He has not left you in the unknown to fend for yourself. Trust in Him more than in your own understanding and abilities.

"Trust in the LORD with all your heart and
lean not on your own understanding; in all
your ways submit to him, and he will make
your paths straight."
—Proverbs 3:5–6

9. *Can I fight for you?*

- In what area of your life are you most desperate for help? In what ways would you like Him to come through for you?
- Have you looked your struggle or battle in the eye? Are you playing offense or defense? How has this played out?
- Have you been striving to fight and defeat this battle on your own? What are some practical ways you can "be still" (cease from striving)? What level of confidence do you have that God can fight and win this battle for you?
- What has been your battle strategy? Have you been putting on the armor of God? Go through each piece of armor and reflect how you can use each piece to fight this battle.

Remember, God *can* defend you, and He *wants* to defend you. He is your advocate; He is for you, not against.you. Read Psalm 91, and remember how He passionately fights for you.

> "Finally, be strong in the Lord and in his mighty power. Put on the full armor of God, so that you can take your stand against the devil's schemes. For our struggle is not against flesh and blood, but against the rulers, against the authorities, against the powers of this dark world and against the spiritual forces of evil in the heavenly realms."
> —Ephesians 6:10–12

10. *Can I carry that for you?*

- Talk to God about the impact this trial has had on you emotionally, mentally, physically, and spiritually.
- Notice if you are worrying (spinning your wheels) or caring (having a clear mind to take steps forward) during this challenging time. What ways can you care more and worry less?
- Have you cast (thrown) your worries and anxieties on Him, or are you tightly holding on to them? What do you need to cast on Him?
- What are some main differences you see between a person who is trying to be helpful in your situation compared to how God can help you?
- Do your actions and emotions reveal that you have more confidence in God's abilities or your abilities to see you through this trial? Name some of these actions and emotions.
- What are some practical ways you can remind yourself of His promises, perspective, and abilities when you're tempted to strive and take control or when the pain becomes unbearable?

Remember, God is gentle, compassionate, and humble in heart. If you feel an insurmountable weight that slows you down and leads to despair, recognize that it does not come from Him. This is not for you to carry. Transfer that weight over to the God of the universe! Cast your cares on Him!

"Do not be anxious about anything, but in every situation, by prayer and petition, with thanksgiving, present your requests to God. And the peace of God, which transcends all understanding, will guard your hearts and your minds in Christ Jesus."
—Philippians 4:6–7

11. *Can I stand in line with you?*

- What have you been waiting for during this trial? What do you hope to have happen? How long have you been waiting for these things?
- What questions or doubts about God's character have come up during your waiting?
- What are some lies that have surfaced about yourself, other people, or God while you are waiting? What is the opposite of these lies (truth/reality)?
- What are some things you have gained from your waiting (e.g., perspective, perseverance, renewed thinking, increased wisdom, new opportunities)?
- Write out at least three promises from the Bible you can anchor yourself on while you wait.

Remember, waiting is not a loss or a blank space. You are not being delayed or denied. God's timing is perfect! Instead of focusing on what He hasn't done yet, place your focus on what He is currently doing, and wait in hopeful anticipation for what He will do in the future.

> "Even youths grow tired and weary, and young men stumble and fall. But those who wait upon the LORD will renew their strength; they will mount up with wings like eagles; they will run and not grow weary, they will walk and not faint."
> —Isaiah 40:30–31 BSB

12. Can I knock your socks off?

- What feels impossible about your struggle? Why does it feel impossible?
- How much hope do you have that this trial will ever end or be redeemed? What words of hope and truth can you speak over this seemingly impossible situation?
- While you're waiting for your "Red Sea" miracle, what "manna miracles" have you seen and experienced so far?
- Make a list of how you've witnessed God come through for you or others in the past. Develop a record of His faithfulness. Do you believe He can do these things again—for *you*?

Remember, even when you don't see anything happening or changing in your situation, it doesn't mean God has stopped working. Keep walking by faith and trusting His good hand and His good heart.

> "Jesus looked at them and said, 'With man this is impossible, but with God all things are possible.'"
> —Matthew 19:26

13. Can I tell you how great you are?

- How have the circumstances of this trial impacted how you view yourself? Are these things true? Have any lies crept in about who you are or your worth?
- What labels have you attached to yourself that don't belong there?
- Have you felt any guilt, shame, or condemnation during this trial? If so, in what ways?
- How have others defined you? How is that the same or different from what God says about you?
- Review the list of your identity in Christ. View yourself from this perspective amid both good and hard times, because this is who you are and how He sees you! Read this list on a regular basis so when Satan tries to demean you, you can tell him who God says you are and that you won't believe anything different.

Remember, as messy as life has been and as weak as you may feel, it doesn't change how God sees you and how He cares for you. No person, situation, or thing can separate you from His love.

> "I thank you, God, for making me so mysteriously complex! Everything you do is marvelously breathtaking. It simply amazes me to think about it! How thoroughly you know me, Lord! You even formed every bone in my body when you created me in the secret place, carefully, skillfully shaping me from nothing to something. You saw who you created me to be before I became me! Before I'd ever seen the light of day, the number of days you planned for me were already recorded in your book."
> —Psalm 139:14–16 TPT

14. *Can I tell you how great I am?*

- How have you seen God work in your hardships so far? How has He intervened? What power and wisdom has He offered you? How has He protected you?
- Review His many names and character traits, and imagine Him being those things in your circumstances. Which names or traits resonate most with you? Are there names and traits you doubt? If so, which ones, and why?
- List out a few areas of struggle in your trial. Then attach a name or character trait of God to those struggles. Believe that God is "being" those things in your struggle.
- How can you view and believe God as less of a "noun" and more of a "verb"—acting and moving on your behalf in your trial?

Remember, regardless of your feelings and emotions or how you view God from moment to moment, He is firm in who He is. He is immovable and unchangeable. This should encourage your heart greatly because even though we're tempted to doubt or walk away, God proves Himself faithful through it all and pursues us when we wander. He's that good.

> "For the LORD your God is God of gods and Lord of lords, the great God, mighty and awesome."
> —Deuteronomy 10:17

15. *Can I be your one and only?*

- How consuming have your recent trials been in your life?
- Who have you reached out to the most for advice and help during your trial? Whose voice holds the most weight, and who do you trust the most?
- What does it look like for God to be "Abba Father" (close and intimate) during challenging and uncertain times?
- What does it look like for Him to be your ultimate source of wisdom and provision?
- Do you have full trust and confidence He can walk you through this trial, leading you to the other side victorious? Why or why not?
- What does it look like to give God the final say and authority to speak into your identity? To view this trial from His perspective and trust Him (not yourself or others) to help you navigate through this trial?

Remember, there is no one like the Father, the Son, and the Holy Spirit. No one else loves you with the same power, wisdom, and grace. For God to be God in your life you have a chioce to make. Your belief needs to "come down off the fence" and say, "Yes, I trust you to be God in my life," or "No, I do not trust you to be God in my life." Which will you choose?

> "Everyone who calls on the name of the Lord
> will be saved."
> —Romans 10:13

Thank you for reading my book.
Thank you for accepting God's invitation.
I pray you always stay hungry.
Smile and rest assured, God is 'being' your God!

Reach out with any comments or inquiries at
publishing.allforone@gmail.com

Made in the USA
Columbia, SC
30 April 2021